Praise for *Coventry Magic*

"We love Jacki and we love this book! She is the real deal and makes candle rituals fun, meaningful, and magical. Her play on words, recipes for change, advice, and down-to-earth spirituality are a joy to read."

—AMY ZERNER & MONTE FARBER, authors of *The Enchanted Tarot* and *The Soulmate Path*

"From self-understanding to healing and transformation, Jacki prepares us to be creators and channels of powerful magic in our own lives. She makes both magical theory and practical application accessible and effective and fun."

—BARBARA MOORE, author of *The Mystic Faerie Tarot* and *Tarot for Beginners*

"Jacki Smith's *Coventry Magic* is a comprehensive book of very practical magic that can be done—with a little practice—by anyone. And it is *effective* magic . . . it works! A very worthwhile book that I have no hesitation in recommending."

—RAYMOND BUCKLAND, author of *Buckland's Book of Gypsy Magic*

"Jacki Smith is a masterful artist of magickal candles. I've enjoyed her blend of strong magickal intentions and great smelling scents in her products. To have her wisdom in a book is a treasure!"

—CHRISTOPHER PENCZAK, co-founder of the Temple of Witchcraft and author of *The Plant Spirit Familiar*

"This book puts Jacki Smith in a category of her own. *Coventry Magic* is much more than a run-of-the-mill magic book; it is a tome of powerful inner transformation!"

—STORM CESTAVANI, host of *Psychic Friends Live*

"*Coventry Magic* isn't just another good book outlining magical practice. It's the best damned self-help book on the market—bar none!"
—DOROTHY MORRISON, author of *Utterly Wicked* and *Everyday Magic*

"Genuineness, applicability, practicality, and power (the ability to affect change) are qualities that are imperative in magical techniques and lore that meet the needs of today's modern magic worker. In this book, Jacki Smith exemplifies all of these qualities. Not only does she provide practical and understandable information, she invites us into her process of discovery, application, and direct results."
—ORION FOXWOOD, author of *The Tree of Enchantment*

"Coventry Magic is more than just a book on practical magic, it is a source book on how to become your magic. This book captures her sassy wisdom, grounded love of the human condition, and magic that actually works."
—IVO DOMINGUEZ, JR., author of *Spirit Speak* and *Casting Sacred Space*

"Jacki Smith provides us with enormous insights, understanding, and wisdom. Reading this feels like sitting with a cup of your favorite beverage and chatting with your favorite feisty, audacious girlfriend as she imparts her knowledge with wicked wit and compassionate humor. "
—GAIL WOOD, author of *The Shamanic Witch*

"Written in a casual, conversational style, Jacki offers not only powerful recipes and spells—including candle magic, spiritual baths, oils, and more—but also the life lessons, guidance, and rituals by which we can use them most effectively!"
—CHRISTIAN DAY, author of *The Witches' Book of the Dead*

"I was delighted to read Jacki Smith's *Coventry Magic*! I have carried her line of magickal candles at my store for years and use them myself with great success. Jacki's humorous and entertaining writing style makes her book completely down-to-earth and accessible, inspiring the reader to experiment with candle magick and understand exactly why the many methods she explains so well work."

—KAREN HARRISON, author of *The Herbal Alchemist's Handbook*

Praise for *Healers Almanac*

"I highly recommend the journey that the *Healers Almanac* will take you on. An individual experience you won't want to miss!"

—DANA M. HAAN, director of The Cincinnati Tarot Guild

"Patty Shaw has a unique voice, perspective, and is a gifted spiritualist unlike any other. You'll learn more than you ever thought possible, and through her meditations, create the life you want most."

—DONNA SAUL, business strategist & consultant

"I make sure I find a quiet moment to read the *Healers Almanac* at the beginning of each month. I love how it follows the cycles of the moon and the natural year. But it is so helpful to have the wisdom of the 21st century goddesses so powerfully written that it inspires me as I read the stories, poems, and the helpful suggestions."

—BRENDA NICKOLAUS, life coach

Do It Yourself
AKASHIC WISDOM

Do It Yourself
AKASHIC WISDOM

access the library of your soul

JACKI SMITH AND PATTY SHAW

WEISER BOOKS

San Francisco, CA / Newburyport, MA

First published in 2013 by Weiser Books, an imprint of
Red Wheel/Weiser, LLC
With offices at:
665 Third Street, Suite 400
San Francisco, CA 94107
www.redwheelweiser.com

ISBN: 978-1-57863-540-5

Library of Congress Cataloging-in-Publication Data available upon request

Cover design by Jim Warner
Cover images: Cosmos sky © Igor Zh / shutterstock;
                Magic book © Vadim Georgie / shutterstock
Interior by Maureen Forys, Happenstance Type-O-Rama
Typeset in Celeste with Franklin Gothic and Futura

Printed in the United States of America
MAL

10 9 8 7 6 5 4 3 2 1

Contents

Acknowledgments

There have been many people who have traveled with us on this journey, or, more appropriately, pushed us down the Akashic path and helped make this book not only a reality, but also helped us sound awesome and smart. From personal friends to authors and clients, this has been a path of discovery and experience. We will never be able to remember and list everyone, and if we've missed you, please accept our apologies.

Thanks to our personal friends who have helped us along this journey: Storm Cestavani, Rhys Hunter, Eve Wilson, Nancy Smith, Diana Mundy, Sue Ustes of Zuzu's Healing Arts, and all of our students and clients.

To our professional guides who we now consider old friends (even if we have never met you); the editors at Red Wheel Weiser, especially Amber Guetebier, who loves us; Robert Taylor, Ted Andrews, Denise Linn, Barbara Y. Martin, Dimitri Moraitis, Amethyst Wyldfyre, Doreen Virtue, Caitlin Matthews, Eckhart Tolle, Linda Howe, Wayne Muller, and all of the authors who have guided our paths.

To our understanding family, who has not only put up the "shhh, they are writing" signs, but also starred in many of our personal Akashic healing sessions. To our parents, Jim and Yvonne Smith, and to all of our siblings. Thanks to Patty's crew, David Shaw, Monica Batsford, Alan Batsford, and to Jacki's crew, the Phoenixes, Tony and Rebecca, and Mary Gilliam.

Preface

C'mon in, the Akasha Is Just Fine:
How Jacki Found the Akashic Records

Everyone wants to claim that they are a "natural born psychic" who comes from a long line of psychics or witches. Well, the only thing I was naturally born with is my red hair (and dammit, I remain a redhead). I can't say that I was a gifted child, or that I saw spirits, or that I could predict plane crashes. However, I can say that I love the spiritual, and I love people. People have always fascinated me; why they do what they do, how they get stuck in their own way, why they love who they love. I consider myself a psychic voyeur; I like to see what makes people tick.

My study around the psychic arts has always been about being the problem-solving go-to girl, the secret magnet, the keeper of all confessions. I worked at developing my psychic skills as an empathic teenager, and if I am being totally honest, I am actually still just a nosey kid who loves giving advice freely. (This has gotten me in trouble more than once, but I've since learned how to harness this, refine it, and be responsible for my words.)

I started with runes and the tarot, practicing on anyone who would sit still for a reading. I taught myself by reading books, picking the brains of other readers I knew, and practicing the craft over and over and over again. I had heard of the Akashic records, but I discounted them because they sounded like too much work, too rigid and too lofty for my hippie self. (Yes, I have always been a lazy witch.)

Meanwhile, Patty (my wonder twin and favorite sister) was bringing to my spiritual table ideas that didn't fit comfortably into my little pagan reality. She brought Jesus, and then I would bring Hekate. She would bring God in all His glory, and I would bring Herne and all the other little *g* deities. We opened up new ideas for each other. Patty started using her newly acquired healing techniques on me, and I showed her how to incorporate ritual into her spiritual practice.

All my studying and training collided, and I soon found myself accidentally in the Akashic records during a reading for a client. "Oh shit, what do I do now?" was my first reaction. But after that I started hearing things more clearly, and knowing things more clearly, and more in depth, than I ever had before. My spirit and mind were open to new, crazier things. The fun had begun.

Not wanting to travel this path alone, I excitedly brought Patty and our friend Rhys into the Akasha with me, and together we did a lot of exploring, trying out of new tools, experimenting on each other, and eventually some great healing work. While Patty and Rhys went deeper into the Akasha as healers, I went out into the waking world and began working with clients.

Now, Patty and I have not only run our business Coventry Creations together for twenty-plus years, we also share an office. It's like we have our own personal healer at a moment's notice, and we still constantly share our discoveries with each other. There are days when we get consumed in the Akasha; where we quickly expand our knowledge, and take our healing to a new level. This book is the result of our unique but also shared experience exploring the Akashic realm together.

To Akasha or Not to Akasha: How Patty Was Drafted into the Akashic Records

It was the late 1980s. I was newly divorced and actively shaking off all the ways being married had mutated me. My focus at that time was on working as a landscape designer, being a mom, building my wardrobe, and barhopping on my kid-free weekends. So you can imagine the sound of my brain cells coming to a screeching halt as a coworker smoothly slipped karma and reincarnation into a conversation over lunch. As my blank stare was met with her look of "Oh you poor dear, you have no idea what I'm talking about!" I had to face the fact that I was still in the dark ages, spiritually speaking.

I immediately slapped myself awake and went to the bookstore and got a good debriefing on the New Age. I powered through those books like they were paranormal romance novels, and I evolved from being an island and a captain of my own destiny to trying on the idea that we are all one and we can (and do) manipulate energy. That magic is not just an illusion, but the act of changing our lives with our own thoughts and intentions. When I learned that we can truly heal ourselves, I knew I wanted to do that with all of my being.

I did what every New Age convert does; I began experimenting on myself. I got crystals to cleanse my aura and balance my chakras, set up altars, took flower essences, figured out my animal totem, got my aura picture taken and analyzed the colors, wore magnets, self-diagnosed and dosed myself with homeopathy and herbal teas, meditated, did yoga, and omed my way into nirvana.

When the dust settled, I found out that I was really good at listening to the silent scream. I could hear, feel, and perceive what was out of harmony in me—and perhaps more importantly, in others as well. That's when I decided to become a spiritual healer. I didn't have a full idea of what that really meant yet, but I was going to find out and define myself as an emotional guru.

Over the next fifteen years I studied with gifted healers and spiritual teachers and refined my own abilities as a healer and spiritual counselor. I learned to read the aura, hear what is not being said, and guide my clients to success through forgiveness, letting go, and reorganizing their energy. I was both challenged by and thrilled with the work. I also earned my master teacher certification in Reiki, became a transformational yoga instructor, started my own healing practice, and wrote a book about healing. I was feeling very accomplished and very spiritual.

I was feeling very accomplished, so what was next? You guessed it; the next phase of my spiritual evolution required me to play in the Akashic records. I had heard of them in metaphysical circles, in books, and from my sisters Jacki and Nancy, but that's as far as I'd gone with them until Jacki's fateful spill into the records in 2005. Of course, I'm talking about the time Jacki suddenly found herself smack in the middle of the records while giving a tarot card reading. That's Jacki for you.

Back in the lab, Jacki suggested my friend Rhys and I try working in the Akashic records using a system she came up with. Holy crap, Batman! All of a sudden our healing sessions were more efficient, deeper, and so very wise. We were floored with how quickly we could move through issues and change the course of destructive patterns that revisited us lifetime after lifetime. We watched with fascination when the energy in the Akasha shifted and changed to support us as we figured out our karma and made new choices. It was magical.

The door to the Akashic records opened to me and invited me to come on in to play and create whatever I wanted to. So I co-created a healing system and found myself at the same time, and it has been much more fun and real than I ever dared to imagine.

This book is a guide to the tools and practices we have learned about the Akashic records over the past twenty years. You can use your own Akashic records to heal and shape your life! And you can access them without fanfare, drama, or intensive initiation. Together we will show you how to get focused, find that door, and open it. We know there are lots of ways to do this and invite you to try our way, but on the condition that once you learn how to you make it your way.

We, along with a whole host of divine beings, will have your back and make it an interesting journey. Stop being a tourist in your own soul, and start being your own caretaker and advocate. This is not a threat or word of caution; we are offering you this personal invitation to step into your Akashic records and use them to create a better life for yourself. In this book we will teach you to enter your records and tune in to a subject you want to explore by using your thoughts and imagination. The records will use your own memories and impressions locked up in your subconscious to jump-start your spiritual journeys and insights. Though we can get to the Akashic records through these other dimensions (which we will explain later), when we skip all that and intentionally go to the Akashic realm we are really in charge, and can dive into the vast information available and play, play, play!

Chapter 1

What's Behind the Door: Akashic Wisdom Unraveled

Throughout this book, we will talk about the many ways your Akashic record room changes and morphs to match your needs. Here is one of Patty's favorite versions of her Akashic record room. She calls it the crystal palace.

> As I walked into my record room I was immediately stunned and impressed by the high glass walls and ceiling. They were crystal clear and leaded. There were tall, lush plants filling the room, and a few exotic birds. (Not too many, because they can be messy.) The furniture was plush, sparse, and tasteful. My records were stored in crystal balls all neatly lined on shelves. Everything about this room was about bringing in and reflecting light. I felt like I was in a giant prism.
>
> I was dressed fabulously as well. I wore a beautiful, flowy gown in light colors with some sparkles. Not too many, I'm not one to be overstated, but some well-placed bling is all I need. The point of this visit was to improve my self-image, and the guides went over the top to help me feel beautiful and full of grace. This experience was unique, as I rarely ask for this kind of attention.
>
> Most of the time my record room is a basic stone structure, like the interior of an ancient temple. There are columns, a

fireplace, a skylight, and bookshelves. I rarely sit, so there is usually no furniture. A tall table will appear if I am going to look at a book. There is always a pond or pool, since floating in the healing waters is my favorite thing to do in my records. My room is typically very plain because it's the best backdrop for all of the crazy visualizations I see there. I get more live action there than in any block-buster movie.

And here is Jacki's first journey into her Akashic records.

I raise my eyes as I enter my library and am astounded by the grandeur. Deep wood shelves filled with well-worn books. Carefully among the books I find trinkets of curiosity, sculptures, tools, and magical items. My eyes light upon comfortable chairs to lose myself in, the per-fect worktable filled with herbs, bottles, and candles, and doors that lead to adventures yet to be known. This is my Akashic record room, and it is mine to discover.

This is the place of perfection, even in its disarray. It's my perfection, a place where I can make a mess and then swish my hands and the mess becomes order. This is a place where all the information I require is available to me; this place feeds my creativity and my passion for life.

In one corner I see a formal sitting area, in another I see my Bedouin tent made of opulent tapestries and pillows to lounge upon. As I travel around the room, I find that I am avoiding the center, looking everywhere but there. This is because in the middle is what is waiting for me to heal.

Yes, I can play in the Akashic records, but then again, I go in there to heal. This is a place of strength and support for me to face the ugly side of my perfection—my personal demons, my fears, and my broken parts. What I discover about myself and my Akashic record room is that truly this is perfect and I am perfect. I will work on what I am ready to, I will get the information that is relevant today, and I can heal at the pace my spirit feels is the best for me. I realize that even though I am experiencing the perfection of the Divine, I still get to be one of the "bad girls" of the Akashic records.

What Are the Akashic Records, Anyway?

The Akashic dimension was created as an interface with the universe or higher knowledge (God) so we can count and recount all of our thoughts, intentions, dreams, actions, relationships, faux pas, successes, karmic credit cards, past lives, sneezes, farts, and coughs. (Don't fret, the records are sworn to secrecy.) Lord knows our brain isn't big enough to hold it all, and there are not enough sticky notes in the world for that magnitude of data, so we have at our disposal the ultimate information backup and retrieval system. It is truly the record of everything.

Akasha is a Sanskrit word meaning "ether, space, or sky." The root, *kash,* means "to radiate or shine." In Buddhism, the Akasha translates as "infinite space," a place that is without matter or any physical consistency. There is no time or space in the Akashic dimension; all timelines exist together simultaneously.

Now Let's Go into the Wayback Machine

The Akashic records concept was the brainchild and focus of Helena Petrovna Blavatsky (1831–91), the founder of the Theosophical Society. In her day, Blavatsky was the clearinghouse for Eastern spiritual thought for us Westerners. Blavatsky created a mother of a bridge between science and religion for us to play upon by uniting all the world religions. She plainly stated that "there is no religion higher than truth," and she believed the secrets of the universe are much grander than anything we have yet to conceive of. She believed that the records could be accessed and manipulated, and that we should do so. In essence, she believed that we use the Akasha and the Akashic records to create the life we are currently living.

You won't find directions on how to access the records in any of Blavatsky's writings, but you will get many lectures on how important it is to develop your paranormal skills and master the esoteric sciences to increase your chances of tuning in to the Akasha. And she makes a valid point. The more you strengthen your psychic abilities and have control over your will, the better you will be able to sustain a valuable visit to your records.

Hundreds of years before Blavatsky was even born, however, many cultures attempted to explain and apply the mysteries of a creative universe in their lives. Through the ages, and in nearly every religion, there have been elaborate stories about a place that sounds very much like the modern description of the Akasha and the Akashic records. The Torah, the Bible, the Koran, the Gnostic writings, the Aquarian Gospel, even Greek mythology all mention a Book of Life in some form or another.

Jewish scriptures say each year on Rosh Hashanah, the Book of Life (which is actually three books) is opened. Everyone will be judged and given an opportunity to atone for their misdeeds before God literally closes the books and inscribes their fate for the coming year.

The Bible also refers to a book or many books in which the activities and motivations of men are documented. In the Old Testament, Exodus 32:32 tells us, "Yet now, if you will forgive their sin—; and if not, blot me, I pray you, out of your book which you have written." In the New Testament, Revelation and Philippians refer to God's book as a record of our actions. Revelation 20:12 states: "And I saw the dead, small and great, stand before God; and the books were opened: and another book was opened, which is the book of life: and the dead were judged out of those things which were written in the books, according to their works." In Philippians 4:3 we find, "And I urge you also, true companion, help these women who labored with me in the gospel, with Clement also, and the rest of my fellow workers, whose names are in the Book of Life."

The legends of the Mesopotamian world included the tablets of destiny where the fate of all creation was discussed and determined annually. The Hittites, an ancient Middle Eastern group, also reference "tablets of destiny." They believed goddesses watched over the birth of their children and declared the destinies of newborns.

The Koran itself is considered Allah's book of remembrance. The prophet Noble Drew Ali wrote: "This age will comprehend but little of the works of Purity and Love; but not a word is lost, for in the Book of Allah's Remembrance a registry is made of every thought and word and deed."

The Aquarian Gospel really brings this idea home in 7:25–26: "This age will comprehend but little of the works of Purity and Love; but not a word is lost, for in the Book of God's Remembrance a registry is made of every thought and word and deed. And when the world is ready to receive, lo, God will send a messenger to open up the book and copy from its sacred pages all the messages of Purity and Love."

In ancient Greek mythology there is a legend that describes the Moirai, or the Fates (Clotho, Lachesis, and Atropos), and how they control people's destiny. Clotho spins the thread (the creation of the life), Lachesis measure out the length of thread (the length of life), and Atropos cuts the thread at the end of life.

What all of these religions and philosophies are pointing to is the idea that there is a divine repository for all knowledge. And through the continual spiritual evolution of the self, each and every one of us can have access to it. If only it were always so easy for the religions of the world to agree!

Twenty-First-Century Akasha

Not having studied Madame Blavatsky's spiritualist writings, nor being Vedic scholars, we embrace the popular twenty-first-century collective understanding of the term *Akashic records* as a place or dimension where we can create new realities, advance our skills, learn life lessons, and heal. A place of our own that we can quickly access through our own energy. We embrace it, and dammit, we feel great about it.

We came to the Akashic records as regular people aspiring to be fully invested in our destiny and the meaning of our lives. And guess what? That search placed us smack-dab in the middle of our Akashic records. At first we didn't go into this great place of knowledge with ceremony and ritual; we bumbled into it, created a ruckus, asked for guidance from the record keepers, healed the obvious, and looked for deeper meaning. We were the bad girls of the Akashic records. We didn't just break the rules; we ignored them and made our own. You gonna tell on us now, or follow along and get a backstage pass to your own life?

This Place Looks Familiar . . .

You've been accessing your Akashic records all these years—and you probably didn't even know it. We use our records in many ways throughout our day, and unknowingly tap into them through other unseen dimensions of consciousness like:

* The dream state
* The unconscious mind
* The subconscious mind
* Meditation, and
* Divination.

The dream state holds many levels of sleep activity and brain activity, with REM sleep being the most talked about. Sleep experts say we need this dream time or REM sleep to download and process the events of our day and make room for tomorrow's events. It's very possible that we download the events of our day right into the Akashic records as we dream each night, and our dreams may even be informed by our records to help us understand our life. If you are stellar at remembering your dreams, you are ripe for being a wizard in the records.

Conversely, when we don't sleep deeply enough to dream, we get a little crazy and may even start to hallucinate. (Maybe you've experienced this if you've ever worked a string of double shifts, pulled an all-nighter to study for an exam, or had the unique feeling of persevering through a too-ambitious road trip.) Not dreaming is a sign that you aren't effectively recording your life into the Akasha, and the last thing you need is blank pages in your record books.

The unconscious is another dimension. It's said to contain thoughts and behaviors of a part of us we don't relate to in our waking life. Carl Jung calls this our storehouse of genetic, mental, and emotional material. This is where we'd find patterns and habits that tell us where we're from and what is influencing us. We also keep models of behavior asleep in our unconscious until we need them to help us get through a situation by playing a specific role. We tend to call them our "inner (fill in the blank)" when we pull them out for use. For example, your "inner warrior" can quickly come out when a loved one is insulted or threatened. Jung called these behaviors archetypes, i.e., the warrior, lover, mother, or guru. If you'd like to understand why you do the crazy things you do, tap into the records and ask the guides what you're hiding in your unconscious.

The subconscious mind is also considered a dimension. In this part of our psyche, all the memories of the fabulous stories we have participated in are categorized and stored for later use. Then, when something comes up, our conscious mind scans our subconscious for any relevant experiences it can draw upon. It uses these tidbits of insight to help us predict how to act or what to expect. All the rest of the information and reactions to events get thrown back into the subconscious to ferment. It's the same with the Akashic records. All the cool information is held in storage until you have a need or use for it.

The Akashic dimension can also be accessed through a transitional meditative state and our desire to know something. We can make the leap to the Akashic records with our will and our emotions, and opening that door to the Akashic field is a matter of tuning in and stepping through. We'll show you a couple meditations to prepare you to enter the Akashic realm in the course of this book.

We can also use divination tools like the tarot, palmistry, astrology, and oracles to prime our psychic pump and get in that Zen space that puts our ego to sleep so we can receive inspirations and impressions from the Akasha. Later, in chapter five, after we've covered the rules and regs, we have a beautiful meditation for you to enjoy. The High Priestess from the tarot will guide you into your records for a looky-loo.

Yes, accessing your Akashic records is as easy as that. Swear to the Akasha. They are your records, and you've been connecting to them throughout your days without even knowing it. Since you are already in touch with your Akashic records unconsciously, why not do this deliberately and get all the "bennies" of dipping into your own spiritual well?

The Perks of Visiting Your Records Often

There are many wonderful benefits to getting to know your way around the Akashic records. You can check out the probable outcomes of a decision you are strongly leaning toward; you can take a vacation and never leave the farm (just what a budget-conscious traveler needs); and you can get the inside scoop on any challenge you are facing, whether it's about money, love, or your health. In addition to these notable perks are the very cool and invaluable benefits of visiting your past so you can learn from your mistakes, tap into the genius of others, and design a life that reflects the real you and fulfills a destiny.

Aren't You Crafty!: Co-creating the Life You Want

The records are much more than recordings of our lives; they are also where we are invited to make things happen. The energy in the Akasha is waiting for you to place your impression upon it, put your ideas in motion, and actively co-create your life.

If we look at the Akashic records as the source of energy that all things are created from, then it follows that when you access it, you are actively taking part in co-creating with divinity. When you move into the Akashic realm, you are entering the oneness, the place of the Divine. Take a minute and digest that one. . . . We will go over it again slower to make sure you get the full power of this statement.

1. The Akashic records are the place where the Divine communicates with you.

2. The records are both historical and potential.

3. You have an all-access pass to explore and learn from your records.

4. When you are in there, you are co-creating your own life very deliberately with the Divine—so make it good!

The energy of the Akasha is very sensitive to your thoughts and intentions. It's a lot like throwing a pebble in the water: Your thoughts touch the energy of the Akasha and ripple outward, find an energy pattern that resonates, bounce off of that, and return to you with more of what you seek.

Speaking of the Past . . .

To co-create with your Akashic records and align yourself with a desired outcome or a potential future, you have to understand how vast your records are. Within your personal Akasha are the records of your soul's entire existence. Let's say you've lived one hundred past lives. Well, you're gonna need a really big record room. (Just imagine, there are billions of people on the planet with hundreds of lives each—what must the breadth and width of the Akashic realm be?!)

By now the idea of reincarnation is as commonplace as cutlery, so we will assume that we are all open to the idea that we have lived many different lifetimes. In our vastness, we, the collective people throughout time, need a place to park our past lives so we can go around the wheel again, unfettered by the past. Every life begins anew, bright and full of hopeful possibilities.

Standing in Each Other's Funk: We Can All Be Geniuses

In Africa it is said that when you stand in the presence of a shaman, you are privileged. This is because you will be absorbing his energy, or "funk." The funkier the shaman, the more healing you can get. Akashic records work on a similar principle because all the rooms are linked—yours, mine, Barack Obama's, your future children's, your mother-in-law's, your ancestors'. How closely they are linked is determined by your sphere of influence. The more intimately your life touches another, or the closer you are to their funk, the more immediately they react to your actions, and vice versa.

There are also links between records that share a common goal or interest. For example, if you are studying the piano, you can access the records of accomplished piano players and experience their level of passion, dedication, and struggle. You can tap into their approach and learn some new skills to add to your own. You can literally mine the records for ideas, tricks of the trade, and techniques to help you improve your own skill level.

✒ A Tip from Aunt Patty

Whenever I am helping a client who's hit a rough patch in a relationship, I look at the Akashic records that connect the two individuals. Together we look at the couple's shared past lives, and how those events may be leaking into their present relationship. Unresolved karma and conflict from another lifetime can contribute to the problems they are having now. Knowing that records are linked gives me the ability to show my client a deeper root cause and, ideally, a solution.

The records hold the light of knowledge of all things. When you expand your spheres of influence and knowledge base, you can peek into or link to other records. From there you can become inspired, create new ideas, change the course of your life, and hey, maybe the lives of others too. For instance, if you are studying quantum physics and you continue to read the teachings of Albert Einstein and Niels Bohr, you are entering their sphere of influence. The knowledge that Al and Niels acquired is stored in their Akashic records, which can inspire your Akashic records. That is how collective knowledge works.

Before you hurt yourself by thinking too hard on this, remember: Your experience of the Akashic records is limited by your knowledge base. Our brains need one lesson to build upon the next to get us to the place of inspiration. You can be inspired to create a master work of music, but if you cannot play an instrument, you cannot communicate this inspiration. Inversely, a proficient pianist can easily access their inspiration and bring a masterpiece to the world. When you are learning something new, you can access the collective knowledge of it through your Akashic records and learn it that much faster.

Use Me, but Don't Abuse Me

The Akashic records are tickled pink to be used as your own personal toolbox for building life skills, gaining wisdom, and making crazy accurate predictions for your next move. If we work at it, the list below demonstrates what we can find out from our records:

* What we need to do to get healthier, lose weight, become more energetic, become clearer thinkers

* Why our life is the way it is right now, and how to make it better in the most efficient and painless way

* How to find a fulfilling career and make more money

* Who our soul mate is, and how to find them

* What we need to do to overcome our fears and take the risks in life that we know will enrich our experiences
* How to accept our limitations and be at peace with them, and let them create strength of character instead of weakness and resentment
* What our addictions are feeding, and how to finally satiate and calm that beast

Unfortunately, the search for meaning in our life often starts with failure or disappointment, illness, hopelessness, or a loss of love, money, or credibility. Somewhere, someone declared that we learn best through pain. Was there a quorum on that motion? We demand to see the documentation. So, when pain is the stimuli, we want real answers and fast. We don't blame you at all, and we believe looking for your answers in your records will turn your perceptions inside out. You will see your failures become lessons, disappointments will become opportunities, and all that illness, hopelessness, and loss will begin to make more sense. Sure, we can try to bargain with God to get what we want, or temper tantrum our way to the prize (let us know how that works out for you), but what will be gained from that? Abusing the system with our childish ways cheats us out of precious wisdom and fabulous strength of character.

On the lighter side, our Akashic seeking can be about getting inspired, planning our next move in life, or finding guidance on which investment is most profitable. In the records we can also find validation for just being alive (so many of us still need that), spiritual guidance (all of us still need that), and the plans for our next million-dollar idea.

Even when we aren't totally clear about what we are going for, our guides will tirelessly steer us toward it because they understand what we still need to learn, what drives us, our hopes, goals, dreams, and aspirations. They know our soul and what our journey is about. It's a win-win situation in the records.

✳

If you haven't guessed already, the records really want to be found, which is why you are seeing so many books, classes, and newly discovered experts. As we have been selling, they are easy, accessible, yours, and just itching for an introduction to you, so go get pretty 'cause here they come.

Chapter 2

As the Records Turn: The Purpose of Accessing the Library of Your Soul

In a perfect world, you would be able to walk into your Akashic record room, flip open the exact right book, and find where you went wrong, in chronological order, and a resolution to all of your problems going forward. But because none of us live in that world, we have to work with what we get. You can access all of the answers in the Akashic records, but you have to work for it, as there are as many ways to get to the answers as there are issues.

Let's face it, working for your answers is a human condition. If it were easy, we would never value the results. Case in point, buy your kid an expensive toy and you'll find it broken under the couch. But teach your kid how to earn his own money and buy his own toy and it'll be under glass when he's not using it. Incidentally, your issues are not cookie-cutter—each one comes with a specific set of circumstances. We are all unique individuals, so what worked for Suzie may or may not be what unlocks the mystery for you. Be prepared to fire up your curiosity and creativity as you pursue the answers to your own specific questions.

Every meditation, spell, healing session, reading, and prayer we do is dedicated to easing our struggle and getting to the answers. We are all on a quest to understand our destiny and purpose in life, and we all want to clear out the irritants and smooth out the path. When you add tapping into the Akashic records to your spiritual routine, you bring richness and clarity to your journey. Hey, maybe a few answers, too.

Look with a New Set of Eyes

We experience life in stories. We are, of course, the protagonist—the center of the story—and we're curious about what motivates us to act the way we do. We'll encounter an antagonist, maybe a few. We'll meet love interests, supporting characters, and side-kicks. We'll want to know the backstory of all the parties and the tragedies, and hopefully at some point we'll get to have the happy ending. The stories that we tell ourselves and others are used to prove a point, prove a belief, or get attention. Your Akashic records use the stories, symbols, and messages that are unique to you so that you can relate to its wisdom. When you understand your story from all angles and perspectives, then you can change its meaning in your life.

How many times have you been upset at a friend for a perceived slight, but when you hear their side of the story, you realize you overreacted? How many times have you been upset with someone and you didn't want to hear their side of the story because you knew it would challenge you and maybe change your mind? Stepping into your Akashic records and discovering a different and deeper facet to the story can help you understand that maybe this experience is not what you think it is, and it is for your highest good. Meaning, you are going to do some growing up.

True story: There was a girl (let's call her Betty) who was really mad at her friend (let's call her Matilda) because she wasn't answering her phone or returning Betty's texts or emails. Betty was doing a favor for Matilda that had a deadline, and Betty wasn't sure of the information she was given. In comes another friend (let's call her Sue) who was helping Betty with the project. Matilda saw Sue every day, and Sue kept bringing back to Betty information on how annoyed Matilda was with this process of getting this favor done. Well, Betty was not having any of that and told Sue exactly what she thought of the situation. Betty thought she was speaking in confidence, but Sue told Matilda her version of what Betty was saying. (Ha!) Betty and Matilda were no longer friends after this situation. Matilda was an excellent grudge holder, and Betty was devastated over the falling out. Looks like Sue is the antagonist here, doesn't it?

Let's have a look-see in the Akashic records over this situation. Betty was feeling how Matilda was pulling back from her, but unbeknownst to Betty, Matilda was going through a divorce and Matilda was scared that Betty would judge her. Betty relied too much on the emotional support from Matilda the Strong. Matilda didn't have the strength to be that support for Betty. Sue loved the attention, but she was also caught up in the situation. Yes, if the parties had discussed this with each other, disaster could have been averted. But since that didn't happen, everyone was hurt. Betty carried this terrible grief with her and as a result had a hard time forming new friendships. Betty's healing came when she looked at the relationship on the Akashic level.

After accessing the Akashic records, Betty was able to lovingly forgive Matilda, Sue, and herself. She let go of the pain she was holding on to and began to trust herself again concerning friendships. More importantly, this experience showed Betty that she had been using Matilda as a source of validation. Betty did a lot of healing work to find her validation with the Divine and work with the light rather than looking to others. As painful as it was, Matilda helped Betty grow and evolve. It's an Akashic miracle!

Being able to read your own records and understanding more than one perspective of your story will change everything. Our stories are what make us. They tell us of our fears, blind spots, stubbornness, and commitments, and they are very changeable.

People say the past is written in stone, but it is just as shifty as our future. Our past relies on our memories, and our memories are filtered through all the crap that keeps us separate from our happiness (a.k.a. the Divine). When we change the filter or get rid of the crap, we can change how we view our past and how it affects us. FYI, by "crap" we mean the judgments, prejudices, reactionary emotions, immaturity, negative thinking, jealousy, and broken soul parts; ya know, crap.

Isn't This Supposed to Be about Destiny?

Wanting to know your complete and total destiny is a tall order. Don't ask until you are ready to know. We're not talking about idle curiosity or wanting to have bragging rights about who you'll be when you grow up. Knowing your destiny is a quest of the spirit, not the ego, and the timing of said quest will be clear to you when your spirit is ready to have your full destiny revealed to you. You kinda have to be ready for it emotionally, mentally, and physically. Think marathon training.

You can think of your destiny as a book; the life you're living right now is just one chapter on your path to your complete destiny. What many people are referring to when they want to know their destiny is, "What do I need to do *right now* to make my life better?" That is much easier to find (and stomach) in the Akashic records, but the application of that answer may still be complicated. Working in your own records on a regular basis can give you just-in-time answers which eventually connect you to your answers of tomorrow, next week, and the next ten years.

The Akashic records can also give you a peek into how you got into a particular mess to begin with. Sometimes you just need to know why or how you got into a situation—what you did to deserve drama. (Now that's a good question, and it comes up a lot in our sessions with clients.) Hindsight is twenty-twenty, and you can take advantage of that during a session in the records and look at the choices you made that blazed the path from where you were to where you are today. If you knew then what you know now, would you have made different choices? Finding out the answer to that question through the Akashic records can literally change the course of your life.

Remember Betty and Matilda? They each have their own backstory of why they made their particular choices and what early life damage colored their reactions to each other. In your Akashic records you can find the ways you were damaged and how those wounds are still the driving factor in your life. Then you can actually do something with this knowledge to create a new potential for your future self. We call this "course correcting." It's not changing your destiny as much as taking a few rocks off the path. You will still have your eye on the same prize.

A basic truth about the world is that it operates on a pretty healthy level of chaotic or wild energy. Your life is continually affected by the actions and opinions of others, and no matter how hard you try, it's difficult to anticipate the outcome of outside forces in your life. The randomness of events and your own emotional responses contribute to a life that, at times, doesn't make any damn sense, and that's a bitter pill to take. To gain a modicum of predictability in this chaotic world you can tap into your records to see where your efforts are getting you. In the records you can:

* Find a new piece of information that is game-changing.

* Look for inspiration and motivation to make a change.

* Tap into your well of hidden resources to find the bravery to move forward.

A Brand-New Kind of Crazy

It's human nature and a psychological truth that we want the world to bend to our dysfunction (or as some call it, our will). Rather than doing the work to find our truth, heal, and change for our own good, we want the world to change for us. Here is the rub: when you change your karma with the world, the world changes to meet it. But if you try and force the world to change to fit your fears, it will meet you right where you are with another dose of your fears. You can avoid hitting this brick wall over and over again if you just change the way you see the world and your place in it.

The first step in breaking the cycle of making the same mistake over and over again is to drop those rose-colored glasses and see life around you as it really is, and not through the filters of your own fears. Rose-colored glasses can prevent you from being aware of things you need to know. When you see the truth and are aware of your illusions, you are better equipped to handle your destiny. And bonus, everything looks like it is bending to you. The deeper truth is that you have changed and are responding differently to the world. Strip away your fear and perceived vulnerabilities and you can go for it. Working in the Akashic records will help you know yourself better in this way. It's a brand-new, good kind of crazy.

Chapter 3

The Healer, the Witch, and the Door: Universal Tools in the Akashic Records

Patty (the healer) and Jacki (the witch) found the door to the Akashic realm through their heart chakras. (We always say that this would be a great start to a sci-fi book or video game). Once we got in there, it was up to our curious natures to poke and prod through the records to understand a simple and possibly universal way to work with them. We had to be able to get in, work, and get out again without having to rewrite the script or put out bread crumbs to find our way back. What we discovered is that Hogwarts' Room of Requirement has nothing on your Akashic record room. Everything you need to answer your questions will make itself known at the right time. Isn't that beautiful! If you take a breath and ask a question, you get it answered.

Not only do they answer your questions, your Akashic records provide several tools to make the journey easier. We have found that this set of tools comes in handy, especially in times of confusion, stress, or "what the hell do we do now?" moments. The tools presented here are universal, but this is not an exhaustive list of all you get. It is, however, a very good starter's set.

The Door

Any door you walk through in your waking life informs your expectation of what will be on the other side. There is a big difference between the front door to your home and the front door of the dentist's office. One involves a couch, a remote, and a nice tall glass of something pleasurable. The other involves a bit of Novocain, a drool bib, and your wallet. Different expectations totally.

Nothing happens if you never enter your room, and the door to your Akashic records is the beginning of your journey. Your door's appearance tells a story of what your psyche is expecting to deal with, as this is the bridge between your waking self and your spiritual self. Before you discount its meaning in your trip to the Akasha, take a look at the door you are walking through, as it holds many clues for you.

The door to your Akashic record room my not even be a door. We have had clients who parted a mystic curtain, drew back a veil of beads, stepped through fog, or even crawled into a cave. We have worked wth shamans who walked into a forest and through a tree. We have even had clients jump past the door and just arrive at their record room.

When you step through the door, your conscious is giving up control over your reality to your subconscious, spiritual self. Having a symbol to make that transition releases quite a bit of your resistance and helps you let go of the reality of dirty dishes and piles of bills in your waking life. The type of door you are walking though tells the story of what your subconscious is expecting the experience to be. It may not be what the Akashic records will show you, but it will definitely be the filter through which you process it.

The Room

Once you walk through the door, you have to go somewhere, and the where is your Akashic record room. This is the place we have been talking about! This is your ultimate playground, the place where all questions are answered or uncovered; this is the place that is filled with the imagery and symbols of your soul's journey. Just like your door, your room will look different each time you go in; library, nomadic tent, forest, crystal garden, under the sea—these are all potential settings for your record room. Eventually you will probably settle into a pattern or routine with variations as you evolve or have a special need.

Besides the location, or theme, of the room you are entering, there is also the condition of the room. Are you "underwater" with worry? Did a tornado go through your room, tearing everything up? Is your room filled with cobwebs of confusion that need to be blown out? Or is your room neat and tidy and full of sunshine, with everything in its place, and seemingly nothing to explore?

✒ Decorating Tips from Aunt Jacki

When I go into my Akashic record room, there are always piles of papers and books showing me that I have more to learn and explore. I usually go into an old library with rolling ladders, old books, and tables to spread out on. In retrospect, it looks a lot like Professor Higgins' library in the movie *My Fair Lady*. When I enter my room, I tend to pick up a little, put away things I am finished with, and clear out old habits and outdated news.

Feel free to decorate your Akashic record room a little while you are there; put in things you are working on manifesting, ask for information you are struggling with, and mend fences from your side with relationships that need a little TLC.

There are certain things everyone's Akashic record room should have:

* A place where records are stored
* A place to read the records, such as a chair and table
* Your guides (more on them in a minute)
* Some kind of structure, as in walls, floor, and ceiling

But that's where the consistencies end. No matter what the structure or non-structure of your room, the idea is that you are in a defined space with a perimeter. Just like cats, we feel better and more secure when we have walls around us and floors to stand on. Even though our records are vast, they are finite. They have to be contained in a way that is protected and closed off from tampering by others.

The Records

No point in having an empty record room. Everyone sees the records in his or her own way. We have heard accounts of many different kinds of storage systems: books on a shelf, files in cabinets, supercomputers, talking trees, and glowing spheres. These records contain information on everything you have experienced, thought, and felt and all the people you did it all with. They also document how you handled your lessons, trials, victories, and where you still need more experience. You will also be able to see the agreements you made with others and why. All this will let you know how successful you have been in developing your soul.

Don't worry about trying to actually *read* your records. We often find that even if we see the words, we don't really read them. Rather, we feel and experience them. Your records will teach you through symbols, people, feelings, past lives, etc. We need to give our records a tangible form in our mind's eye, but once you walk through that door, everything you experience is part of your records. The room, the stuff within it, the state it is in, the lighting, everything is part of the message you are getting from the Akasha.

Did you know that everything in your waking life has a record? Even your pets! Need to know why your cat keeps peeing in that same corner of the house? Take a look at little Betsy Wetsy's records and see if you can help her find her litter box. Check out the unwritten history of your home: Look up your address in the records and see if there is anything you need to clear or bless.

We had a friend once who was selling her wedding ring set and wanted to clear anything that would stop someone from buying the rings. While she was in her record room, she discovered the anger, the fighting, and the disappointments between her and her ex-husband were still attached to the rings. Once she was able to clear them of that energy, they immediately sold.

The Guides

Though they probably don't deserve to be called tools (they are much nicer than that), your guides are available to help you explore the Akashic realm. You are free to ask your guides anything, but the quality of the answers you receive will depend on how good your questions are. If the answer you get is in the form of a question, that's a clue that you already know the answer and they are "helping" you remember it.

The guides that are always in the records are: the keepers of the records, the master teachers, and the loved ones. You can count on the presence of these guides every single time you visit your records. Other guides come and go as you need their expertise. For a complete list of potential guides along with their descriptions, see chapter 8.

Healing Waters

One time in the Akashic records we found a pond of sparkling, crystal clear water off to the side beckoning us to take a dip. It was gorgeous, and we were thirsty just looking at it. It's the kind of thirst that can only be quenched by jumping in up to our necks and splashing around. Of course we delayed our spiritual splash and splash to ask the guides, "What gives? This looks amazing, what is the pond for?" We were told, "You need a bath."

We guessed our funk was too much for the guides and they wanted us to tidy up, but that was not the case. We were invited to take a spiritual bath, and the pond was full of healing water that would release all that was pent up inside as pain, both emotional and spiritual, as we floated around. We call this activity "releasing pain bodies"—a phrase we picked up from Eckhart Tolle in his book *A New Earth*. A pain body is old, pent-up pain from the past that you've stuffed down deep rather than release. Your pain bodies can be activated anytime you feel threatened, humiliated, shocked, or depressed—just about any negative emotion. When your pain bodies are up and running, you lose control and can go into a blind rage, trigger deep depression, and basically are not yourself any longer. Our guides picked up on Mr. Tolle's inspiration and ran with it in our Akashic records by providing us with the healing waters and a place to release our pain and detox our spirits. Since you dip into the healing waters after you have done your healing work, pain bodies are pretty easy to let go of.

You may come across a pool, pond, or hot tub in your own Akashic record room that you can use to wash off the pain of the past. It is a fantastic way to release old emotions that get locked up in your aura and body. What's even better, you don't have to re-experience them, analyze them, or evaluate them; just let the pain wash away. Think of it like this: You don't inspect the dirt you are washing off at the end of the day and share memories and stories of how it got there, do you? That would be absurd, and you'd run out of hot water long before the analysis was done. Just like you don't become attached to the dirt on your body, don't continue to be attached to the denser pain bodies you have been carrying around. Let them wash off and be recycled.

The Screen

Taking an objective look at you and your stuff takes time, practice, and an open mind. One way to see things objectively is to put yourself or your questions up on a big screen. You've always wanted to see yourself on the silver screen right? OK all you starlets, this is your curtain call, so be prepared to bare your soul as you let it all hang out, energetically speaking.

Using your imagination, create a viewing room with the big screen. Don't forget a comfy chair and a bag of popcorn, too. This movie's got a sequel *and* a prequel. Now sit back and relax as the drama begins. Try picturing your own body (including energy bodies) on the big screen, or project an image of yourself carrying out a habit you'd like to change. Watch a short film on your relationship, or your past, or potential futures. How you use the viewing screen is limitless.

Take a Look at Yourself

To look at your own bad self, ask for a holographic representation of you in all your glory to be projected up on the screen. This is your "let's see what's under the hood" viewing. Tip: You can turn your holographic image around to see your sides and back, too.

If you are familiar with chakras and auras, you can check them out and assess the quality of the energy by looking at the brightness and clarity of their color. You will undoubtedly also see bits and pieces and parts floating in your aura, and fibers extending out from you and going somewhere. This is your history and evidence of your interactions with people. The floaters, clouds, and streaks of random colors are also telling you about damage to your aura, energy leaks, ideas, people, and events you are hanging on to.

✒A Crash Course in Chakras and Auras

Chakras

Chakras are energy vortexes found in your aura. They spin and make the light your aura pulls in available to you for whatever you are going for in your life. There are seven major chakras, and they line up along a central channel starting at the top of your head, running along the spine and ending at your tailbone. You also have chakras in your hands and feet.

The crown chakra is violet or white and is above your head. This chakra opens as you become enlightened or awaken spiritually.

The result is a life lived in cooperation with spirit, and that's a good thing.

The third eye, or brow chakra, is in the center of your forehead and is indigo or dark blue. In this chakra you process all thought. Spiritually inspired, it is bright and full of light and helps you achieve your goals. I bet you can guess what negative thoughts do for you.

The throat chakra is in the center of your neck and is medium blue. You use this chakra to communicate your thoughts through the power of your words. You can heal, create, or destroy with your tone and the words you choose, so choose wisely.

Your heart chakra is in the middle of your chest and is emerald green. The heart chakra is a workhorse and processes all your worldly affairs. This is also the seat of your soul where all the events of your life are recorded. It is also the opening to your Akashic records.

The solar plexus chakra is just below your ribs and above your belly button, and it is yellow. This is the chakra of your will and determination. A damaged solar plexus can really take the wind out of your sails.

The navel chakra is about an inch below the belly button and is orange. You process your emotions in your navel chakra. Combine the emotions of your navel chakra with the thoughts from your third eye and you've got the power to create.

The root chakra is at the tailbone and is red. Your unresolved conflicts of the past are stored here, as this is your spiritual dumping ground. Clear this chakra out and you'll be feeling pretty free and easy about life.

Your chakras work together as a system. One flat chakra can cause you to have to pull over onto the shoulder for some service. (Hope you carry an extra can of fix-a-flat.) Frequent chakra-balancing and clearing meditations will keep your chakras up and running for many miles.

Auras

There is a field of energy around all living things. We call it the aura. Though not easily seen with the physical eye, it can be seen with the help of Kirlian photography and developed psychic perception. Your own aura is just as important to the vitality of your physical body as good nutrition and exercise. Your aura is also your bodyguard, keeper of your history, and tattletale of your bad habits. The aura extends about the length of your out-stretched arm all around you and penetrates to the core of your spine. It is complex and has many functions. In fact, your aura holds the blueprint for your physical body and is the battery for your vitality. If your aura is depleted, you will feel exhausted and can get sick.

Much of the information we have about the aura has been col-lected by psychics and metaphysicians from all over the world. Famous seers have given detailed descriptions of what the aura looks like and what it does. For the most part your aura supports your life and keeps your body healthy by pulling light from your higher self and feeding it to every aspect of your existence. This means your thoughts, your emotions, your physical body, and your soul.

You can literally heal your life and your body by keeping your aura full of light and constantly releasing negative energy. This is best achieved through prayer and meditation, but also through proper nutrition, exercise, and a good attitude.

It's true; you can't afford the luxury of a negative thought. Anger, unresolved grief, hatred, and resentment all damage your aura and reduce its ability to bring light to you. No light means no life. This is why we always look at the aura during healing sessions. The aura tells us the story of your life and how well you are han-dling your challenges.

All this information is invaluable in the self-healing of your energy body. A general rule of thumb during this maintenance looky-loo is that you can only clear what is already healed. If you find something that won't budge, you'll need to work on it with a trained healer. If that happens to be you, then go for it, but be aware that it's often difficult to heal ourselves because we lack the objectivity needed to keep us from reacting or becoming judgmental. (By "reacting," we mean getting caught up in the emotions that ruled you when the thing that messed you up in the first place happened. By "judgmental," we mean only seeing your point of view and dismissing any wrongdoing on your part and placing all the blame on someone else, both of which will cause you to be blind to the truth that is here for you to experience.)

It's during this viewing that you can call upon your guides to clear your aura and chakras and sever any unhealthy attachments you have to people (or they have to you). If the attachment won't clear, you may have an agreement or karma that you are working out with that person. You can take this to a healer or let it work itself out over time. We find Archangel Raphael an invaluable ally for clearing and polishing. He is the all-purpose healer and our go-to just about every time we go into the records for some R and R—rest and repair, that is.

If healing and clearing are new concepts for you, don't worry—we'll come back to these ideas later on in chapter 7.

Back to the Future

You can also use the viewing screen to look at your past lives, future lives, and parallel lives. You can even look at your childhood and recover gaps in your memory to help you heal traumas that are still affecting you today. This is particularly difficult to do alone, and we highly recommend seeking out the assistance of a shaman or spiritual counselor. But if you'd like to take a peek at who you were or will be, or would like to know why you are afraid of heights, ask your guides to put the whole scene up on the screen, and watch it like it's a movie. This is a great way to become the objective observer. The distance helps you view everything without doubt, hesitation, or fear. It will also help you ask more pointed questions about what's going on as you explore your records in depth.

✒ Akashic Tips from Aunt Patty

I'm not the greatest sleuth around, so I can get easily frustrated in the Akasha. When I am particularly stumped, I ask my guides to show me what they want me to learn in a different way. They already sense my frustration, but hold back until I ask for help. They would rather I work through my frustration and figure it out than blurt out the answer. This helps me build my skills as a problem solver and deepens my confidence in myself. But they are not there to tease me, so when I need help, they give it. Sometimes the best way through is a well-worded question.

Your movie will sometimes stop and pause, almost appear stuck. When that happens, ask for the next important scene you need to see to be queued up. We find that this happens when our clients start to lose focus or they are feeling afraid. It's like they emotionally put on the breaks till their processes and reactions can catch up. If you find this happening a lot, you can try to wait it out, come back another time, or stop and make an appointment with your healer practitioner. Remember, do what you can, have fun, and ask for help when you need it.

Creating Tools on the Fly

There are many more tools that we use in the Akashic records, but we don't use them all the time. The few times we needed them nothing else would do, and now we have them in our Akashic tool box for a client or for teaching purposes. These tools are kind of like your Halloween costumes; they are perfect for the moment but they don't need to be kept in the front of your closet year-round.

The symbolism you experience in the Akashic plane is your Rosetta stone for understanding the energy that exists there. Everything has meaning, and all the symbols can get very confusing. Your most important tools in the Akasha are: your problem-solving and curiosity (asking questions) and your imagination. Over and over we say, "The Akashic records communicate through your imagination using the language of your experiences." This is where your imagination and experiences come together to create the tools you need to facilitate your healing on the fly. This is where we give you permission to make things up as you go.

Making things up does not include the story shortcut "and then they woke up and this never happened." That's just cheating, and cheating will get you sent right back to the beginning to deal with this situation a second time. (Denial ain't just a river in Africa, honey.) When we say "making it up," we mean including a wizard who puts the offending magic in the cauldron of flames to destroy it totally.

Your Akashic record keepers will help you with this. Ask for help, ask for hints, ask for intercession. Ask for the right tool at the right time, and then step out of the way as it is created. What you want to do is relax and not judge what is coming to you. It will make sense eventually.

We have seen tornadoes sweep away the cobwebs of confusion, and tidal waves wash away the old beliefs that were cluttering up a room. We have watched trees uproot the bones of an old family legacy, and clay pots hold the light of a soul damaged by a difficult situation. There are lots of symbolic tools you will see and create in your many Akashic journeys. Enjoy them and journal about them to give you a deeper insight when you review them later.

Never the End

Play with the tools we have listed here; get to know them, and then you will understand that more tools will be created for you or by you. Don't limit yourself to these, and absolutely ask your keepers if there are any new tools that will help you through a lesson that you are having trouble completing.

Chapter 4

The Rules and Regulations of the Akashic Records—How the Records Work

Isn't it irritating? You join a new club that looks very promising, and the first thing that happens is they slap a bunch of rules on you. Talk about a killjoy. Not only that, we said we were the bad girls of the Akashic records and we ignore all the rules. The truth is that while we *are* bad girls, there are some universal truths that we need to share with you before we send you headfirst into the Akasha.

Consider these rules and regs to be your safeguards as you venture into a place capable of changing your entire world. Even though we brag about our rule-breaking tendencies, these rules will actually help you enjoy and get the most out of your trip. So, wait behind the dotted line, keep your hands in the car please, and enjoy the ride.

Rule 1: Your Records Cannot Be Tampered With

The records are more protected than anything; they can't be changed or destroyed without your permission. Seriously, it's just not possible. Even the gods can't tamper with your records. Oh and by the way, your divine allies only work with your records when you call them to. Yes, you can muck around in your own records, but there will be supervision from the record keepers, and this is for your own protection. Be assured, your Akashic record keepers won't let you delete yourself, and they will let you know in no uncertain terms when you are trying to change something that is not ready yet (too bad we don't have a keeper for our computers). Others can and will affect your waking life, and you'll find each and every one of those events recorded in your records, but no one else can waltz in and rifle through your stuff. So play around all you want knowing that your records are secure and you can't screw them up—and in fact no one else can, either.

Ghosts in the Record Room

Speaking of others being in your record room, don't worry when you see someone you know in your records. It's all smoke and mirrors. What you are seeing is a representation, a holographic image, if you will; they are not really there. It's really important to have confidence in this fact when you come face-to-face with your antagonist or abuser. It may look like them, and you may feel those same old feelings when you come face-to-face with them, but they are not really there. Go ahead, put your finger in their eye. It won't hurt. In fact, go ahead and yell at them, give them what they gave you. They will be clueless, and an exercise in cathartic release may help you. The real reason their image is up close and personal is to show you that there is still something you need to learn about yourself, and Spirit says this is the perfect person or situation to help teach you. We apologize for the New Age mumbo jumbo, but this style of healing really works.

So please use this opportunity to get tons of information from this holographic image. Some of it will come from observing the image, and some of it will come from your guides as they help you be objective and broaden your awareness. It seems magical, but it's more about being non-judgmental as you review the event again from a higher perspective.

Although you are in your records to promote healing and make changes in your waking life, there will be no skipping out on karma and lessons to be learned. This is also part of rule 1. There is no tampering with your own records to skip over necessary experiences of the lesson (*psst,* that's called cheating). Lessons need to be learned and integrated, and to do that you need to take it one step at a time. If you do manage to pull this off, you will go back and do it again. No deed goes unrewarded. But alas, this is how we evolve our soul. Even if it feels painful and disappointing now on a soul level, it's totally OK, because we want to experience and learn everything. It's exciting to our soul, and it wants to evolve. Our human personality is often frightened or threatened by these adventures or whines because it takes too long. Immediate gratification is not always the best way to go, and if we skip out on the lesson, we cheat ourselves out of some pretty spectacular wisdom. Life's a game, and the universe won't advance you until you've earned it. Besides, the Akashic records themselves are enough of a cheat code. Any more, and the game gets boring.

Rule 2: No Mucking Around in Other People's Records

We are all connected, whether you believe that or not, and mucking up or even tweaking someone else's records will impact you and your future. So don't even think about it. You can tap into and see others' Akashic records as they intersect with your own, but that is the limit of your exploration. No manipulating, cursing, hexing, jinxing, coercing, or modifying someone else's feelings or actions in any way is allowed.

We know, wanting to fix your spouse's bad habits may be the reason you are studying the Akashic records. But everyone has free will to be as brilliant or as stupid as they want to be, and besides, the guides don't let you meddle in other people's files. Everyone is protected, even your enemies and family members.

Honestly, once you start mucking around in your own records you will learn how life really works, and it's quite a game changer.

A Tip from Aunt Jacki

One time I tried to influence my husband and daughter to see things my way by way of their records. I wanted to make our upcoming move happen faster, and I wanted to see why they were dragging their feet on making a change that would benefit us all. When I tried to take a peek at their records, NO ENTRY was the image I got for both of them. I thought that was hilarious. The guides had heard my intentions loud and clear, so I went back to my own records to ask a new question.

I asked, "What do I need to learn about myself through my husband and daughter's resistance to moving?" After much healing work, it came down to role reversal; I needed to move from catering to their wants to standing up for my own needs. Once I asserted myself and explained why I thought it was important that we move, *now*, everyone was able to get on board with little to no resistance. It was all in my perspective.

Reading Other People's Records: You Can Look, but You Cannot Touch

True, you cannot alter someone else's records, but you can take a peek on two conditions: 1) If what you are looking at pertains to your own records, or 2) someone has asked you to look at their records and you are a professional peeker.

We are social creatures, and our interactions with others define who we are and what we believe. And, let's face it, our actions can do a lot of damage. When we explore our relationships, we often get a peek at their records, their pain, and their reasons why. If you like the other person, you can always ask their higher self if they would like you to help them with their healing. If they say yes, they will experience the same healing as you. If they say no, then bless them and send them on their way—because really, this healing or investigative session is all about you anyway.

If you don't like the other person, getting a peek at their inner workings can give you a better understanding of why they act the way they do. That understanding helps you let go of your own pain within the situation and heal more fully, and it may help them heal as well. Whenever you have the opportunity to empathize with others in your life through the Akashic records, you get another opportunity to develop more compassion.

Rule 3: If You See It, You're Ready to Deal with It

As the old saying goes, you will not be given more than you can handle. If you look at the inverse of that; when you are ready to handle it, you will get it. The keepers of the Akashic records are not only super smart, they are perceptive, and they know exactly what you can handle and exactly what you are ready to deal with. When you step into your records, you will get exactly what you are ready to work on. Be content with that for now; for when you are ready for that next level of healing, it will be offered up on a silver platter. For all you overachievers and workaholics, what you get in the moment will be enough to handle. Trust us.

Let's say one day you can no longer tolerate the cap being left off the toothpaste. You know your spouse does it subconsciously and habitually, but it's still a problem for you. Or let's say you unexpectedly start developing hives every time you hear televangelists give their ministry. This is a sign that you are ready to deal with the issue that these behaviors represent. When you start obsessing over something, the underlying issue is bubbling up to the surface and a trip into your Akashic records is in order to find out the key to resolving it. These spiritual triggers can:

* Play out in your life over and over again, eventually resolving themselves,

* Become intolerable, forcing you to change to tolerate them, or

* Inspire you to take authority over your spiritual beliefs and see what thorn is in your psychic side.

We lovingly call the Akashic records our room of necessity, because that's really how it works. It's what you need it to be when you need it. Every time you go into your records, they will be slightly different; what is essential to see, hear, feel, and know will be there and be made available to you as you are ready for it. Never has there been a better place to hang out than in a room that manifests the tools you require to heal, create, and learn when you desire them.

One would think with the vast, unending energy of the Akasha it would be easy to get lost, but you actually can't get lost in there. You can only go where you are invited. You can only see what's relevant to a particular session, and thank the keepers that this is so, or else your brain would fry and you would have to ask Hansel and Gretel for their spare bread crumbs to find your way out.

We do have to break some potentially disappointing news to you here. The download of information you get while in the records is designed to be just enough to inspire you. There is no "speeding the process along" to become an instant expert in the Akasha. You will not suddenly become a virtuoso after a year of piano lessons and a few trips to the Akashic records, but what you will get, if you ask, is good, solid inspiration that tells you that your choice to become a musician is real and you can do something with it if you keep on going. While in the records let the emotions, hard work, insights, and accomplishments of others speak to you and your experiences. If you wish, ask your Akashic guide to assist with some specific challenges you are having, but remember, you have to start with common knowledge. You still need to know how to read music if you are going to talk shop with Beethoven and Mozart. No shortcuts.

A Tip from Aunt Patty

When you find that you are getting information that seems beyond your skills, it's a hint that you are still remembering what you know and where you've been. Allow yourself time to heal whatever you have put in your way to stop you from realizing your full potential. This is a process as well. Doing the work and taking each step is the way we learn. If you have forgotten something, it may be that you need time to regroup and look at things from a new perspective. You may also need to do some forgiving.

Rule 4: You've Created Everything in Your Records

Everything you see in your records was created at some point by your free will, either in this lifetime or in a past life. The changes that take place in your records are the ones dictated by your actions, agreements, karmic connections to people, fears, regrets, and expectations. If you don't like what you see and want a different reality, you'll need to do some un-creating and healing. All of your own free will, of course. Gee, that makes you responsible for everything, doesn't it? Accepting responsibility for all aspects of your life may seem overwhelming, but in reality it is freeing. If you created it, you can change it. Now that's a rule we can get behind.

As we've stated, nothing changes in your Akashic records without your request and permission. You have Akashic record keepers and other divine beings in your records, but they can't and won't take action without your consent. Your free will is greatly honored and protected, as is your wisdom and process of evolution. This is why you won't be going into your records and expecting to be told where all the closets with skeletons are. Nor will you be told what to do with the skeletons when you find them. Your experience in the records is for you and you alone, and to have all the mystery taken out is to treat you like you're stupid. And we know for a fact that you are not stooopid.

The Rest of the Story

Once you make a decision to change something in your personal Akasha, you have to make a behavioral change in your waking life too. If you don't follow through on your promise in real life, you can easily undo all the wonderful work you've done in the Akasha and perpetuate your spiritual wounds. Maybe you've vowed to not judge yourself so harshly, make better food choices, or forgive the people who've hurt you in the past. It's not until you literally do what you say you're going to and create new habits that the energetic changes you made in your records will be able to support you. What Spirit is asking of you is to be a partner and choose to do in your waking life what you were willing to do in your imagination, a.k.a. the records. Your next question needs to be, "How am I going to use information from the Akasha in my daily life?" That is the secret to your success in overcoming your issue.

Our wounds are deep-seated, so don't expect to solve every issue immediately. You are wounded in layers, and you will heal in layers. As we stated in rule 3, you will be given only what you are ready to see, and that includes healing too.

🖋 Life Lessons from Aunt Jacki

I have several stories in my cache that show exactly what to expect when you don't support in your waking life the healing work you do. One particular issue I'm still working on is healing my weight challenges. I've resolved to change my attitude and actions when it comes to food many times in the Akasha, but when I didn't follow through when it came to what I actually put in my mouth and why, there was backlash. In disrespecting myself in this way I didn't just undo the Akashic healing I'd experienced,

I created brand-new issues. I go back to square one on this issue each time I do a healing unless I create a spiritual habit. What I have done with recent healing sessions is ask my guides to clear the old spiritual habit and help instill a new one. It works!

Making changes in our Akashic records is like planning a to-do list. Planning is important; nothing would get done if we didn't plan our actions first. But you also have to come out into your life and follow through, put tab A into slot B and do the work. You can figure out how to remove the blocks, but you still have to walk down the path.

🖋 A Tip from Aunt Patty

I had a client whose main reason for seeing me was to get help restarting his career. Time and time again he'd leave the sessions hopeful, but he'd return the next week dejected because no one had called him for an interview. My client had moxie, and he knew that once the boss met him he'd be in like Flynn.

Then I asked him, "Did you send out any résumés this week or call anyone about scheduling an interview?"

"Well, no!" he'd say. "Spirit told me through at least three psychics that such-and-such company should be calling me any day now."

"When did you get this prediction?" I'd ask.

"Hmmm, about a year ago, after I sent them my résumé."

Lots of blocks can be removed surrounding a desired outcome, but you have to do the heavy lifting to make things happen. Follow up in real time, and you may find that things move faster and you'll get where you're going sooner.

Rule 5: Your Past Lives Do Not Excuse Bad Behavior

From time to time we need to go into the past during healing sessions to resolve events, emotions, and fears from long ago. Our past lives can give us clues when the challenges we face today makes no sense in this life. We can visit these lives and bring forward the gifts from that time, meaning the things we've mastered, and the love we've experienced, to help us today.

A past life can be a road map as to how you got to this life, or a catalog of repeating patterns and habits. But whatever happened in your past lives, they are never an excuse to give up, hate on another person, or say that you were just meant to be that way. If a past life makes itself apparent to you, it is because there is something to resolve.

✒ Past Life Lessons from Aunt Patty

A charity event was looming, and I was sick as a dog. I didn't want to drop out, so I went into my Akashic records to see if there was a woo woo reason for my illness. Of course there was. I found a past life where I was a nightclub singer who drank and smoked to much. In that life I wasn't happy because what I really wanted to do was move to Paris and paint. I stayed a night club singer because I could make money at it, and I blew off my designs on going to Paris because I couldn't give up the career that kept me in diamonds and furs. Yep, I was a sellout. In this lifetime, as I prepared to step under the bright lights again, all that jazz from the past life came flooding back and my body responded with symptoms that just wouldn't clear up. Talk about a hangover. I did some healing and closed the door on that past life and was able to participate in the charity event. Actually I did look like I was drunk, but it was the cold medicine, I swear.

Denise Linn (*www.deniselinn.com*) does an amazing seminar on past lives where you go to a life and bring back a trait or skill that you admire and are lacking in this life. She guides you to leave the rest of the life in the past, where it belongs, and bring forward the qualities that can help you now. This is an energetic memory, and if you work at it, take lessons, and practice your skills, you'll progress quickly, as if you are remembering how to do it. Kind of like riding a bike!

Don't get too wrapped up in the rules, as they are in effect whether you agree with them or not. We call them rules to give us the feeling that we follow them willingly rather than them being the "forces of the Akasha" that they really are. Calling them rules or laws gives us the impression that they can be broken, but, alas we are not that cool. Even the bad girls are subject to those rules, or forces of nature. As you travel your own Akashic journey you will bump up against these rules just as we did. At least now, you have been forewarned.

Chapter 5

Getting Intimate with the Records

Your connection to the energy in the Akasha is the most intimate relationship you can have. The Akashic records are where you will receive unconditional love, gentle guidance, and inspiration to help you through your life without fail, and there is no better way to access this wisdom than through your heart. Creating and nurturing a connection with your records are the point of this book. This is possible for *everyone*. We have successfully guided hundreds of folks into their Akashic records, and every last one of them got there. All are welcome!

We literally fell into the process of getting into the Akashic records by moving through the heart chakra, and when it happened, we were so excited and in awe. It was humbling to be shown this information and to be a part of our client's personal transformation. It is the connection that enables us to access our own records and then other people's records.

Your heart chakra is your seat of unconditional love and compassion and is designed to transmute energy from one quality into another. When you are immersed in this vibration, you can access your records more fully, with rapt attention and the least amount of judgment.

It makes perfect sense to enter your records through your heart. Not only is the heart a place of inner peace and truth, it is also the place where all healing begins, as represented by Tiphereth on the Tree of Life. Tiphereth is the center sphere that is connected to all the spheres. It is governed by the nurturing Archangel Raphael (more on him later).

Connecting to the records through your heart will protect you from recycling your illusions and delusions (no one needs the repeat of that). It also protects you from tipping into the chaos and crazy of the world or astral plane.

Note: The astral plane is a dimension that holds all of our thoughts, feelings, and abandoned potential futures; it's basically our psychic dumping ground.

Robert Taylor, host of the Grosse Pointe, Michigan television show *Out of the Ordinary into the Extraordinary* and paranormal psychic, did a reading party for Jacki where he used a system of reading from the Akasha. This was her first introduction to the Akashic records. Robert got his training in India, and at the time he was one of a few in the whole country who could do this kind of Akashic reading—it was phenomenal and complex. We never thought we'd be able to do what he did and look where we are now! We may not be using his methods, but we're finding our way to the Akasha nevertheless.

✒Akashic Tales from Aunt Jacki

When I take clients to their Akashic records, I ask them to pay attention to their heart chakra and let it become a brilliant green room. In the center of this room is a door and door frame—no walls. I show them that they can walk completely around the door so they know that door takes you to another dimension. I caution them to pay attention to how the door looks and how hard or easy it is to open the door. Once they open the door, my clients walk right into their Akashic record room. Every single one of my clients has been able to go through, and it is that easy and effortless.

✒A Tip from Aunt Patty

Guiding clients to their Akashic records is an exercise in imagination. We all love to dream and visualize wonderful images and stories. The journey into the Akashic records is like that, and a little pomp and circumstance just make it juicier. If you can create a picture in your mind, you can find your way into your records; you just need the right cues and suggestions. Your unconscious will take care of the rest. I also like to use the heart chakra for the access point. It's our own power center that vibrates peace and balance. When we allow ourselves to be peaceful, it is easier to connect with the Akasha. Going into the center of your heart chakra surrounds your consciousness and ego with a calm beauty that lets worldly concerns fall away and you can begin to experience the grander part of yourself.

Accessing Your Akashic Records the Quick and Dirty Way

There are as many ways to access your Akashic records as there are people. But if you are like the bad girls of the Akasha (that's us), you'll want to learn the quick and dirty way first. It's not really "dirty" per se; it just gets you where you want to go *tout de suite*. (For those of you who are more into playing by the rules, a formal introduction of connecting to the Akashic records can be found on page 55.)

Balancing Your Energy

Before doing any meditation, it's a really good idea to balance your energy. What you are really doing is releasing all the ways you are exhausting yourself by leaking vital energy through hooks, drains, bad moods, anxiety, and babysitting other people's broken soul parts (more on that in later chapters) from your aura and chakras. You are also using this meditation to get into your body.

We bet you didn't know that you spend a majority of your time with your energy (aura) up in your head, off to the side, or trailing behind you. When your body is not centered in your aura, you could say it's like the lights are on, but nobody's home. It's really hard to get anything done when you are distracted or asleep. Grounding and balancing your energy are the key to a successful visit into the Akashic records because you will be mentally, emotionally, and spiritually present. Here we go.

First, get comfortable: Put your feet on the floor, place your hands open on your thighs, and relax your neck.

Take a long inhale, counting to three; as you exhale let your shoulders drop.

Take another three-count inhale and let your chest open, forcing your shoulders to drop further.

Take a third long inhale, counting to four. As you exhale, allow your attention to drop to your feet. Feel all of the energy that you walk through every day drop to your feet. Everything that has been said to you, all the agendas and expectations others have for you drop to your feet, filling them with energy that is tingly, hot, and a bit uncomfortable.

All energy that doesn't belong to you drops with each exhale. And with each inhale that energy is pushed down.

As your feet start to feel full and heavy, imagine the chakras at the bottoms of your feet open up and dump all this excess energy into the earth to be cleansed. The more it drains out of you the more it pulls on all of this energy that is not yours and pulls it out of your body.

Now you can see your connection to the earth; all the crud and gunk that was blocking it is now clear. Your connection is strong and pulsing, and your body responds by gobbling up all this energy and putting it to use by energizing you in a calm and relaxed way. Your connection to the earth is always there, always on, and it's just the junk from everyday living that can limit its flow of power to you.

The earth energy flows up through your lower chakras and into your heart chakra, where it is pumped out to every cell, every nook and cranny in your body. Dark spots are cleared. The earth energy continues on up to your head and touches your scalp.

Extend your breaths to a count of five. Take a few deeper breaths, and on your third exhale allow your attention to rise to the top of your head, your scalp. Every five-count breath shakes loose those inner critiquing voices, and they float to the top of your head like bubbles. Your own agendas, self-talk, expectations, to-do lists, disappointments, all float to the top of your head with each breath. You scalp starts to feel tight and tingly.

As these things float up, the pressure on your scalp builds to the point where your crown chakra blossoms open to release all this junk into the sky for cleansing. Faster and faster it pours out, pulling with it the things that you hid from yourself that would sabotage your connection to your Akashic records.

As these things drain away, you can see and feel your connection to the Divine. It is always there, but sometimes it's gummed up by your own junk and personal expectations. Divine energy feels tingly and light as it filters down your upper chakras to your heart chakra. Your heart pumps it out into the rest of your body, down your lower chakras, and out to all of your cells and DNA. This divine energy fills in all the dark spots and illuminates them with your divine essence.

The earth and divine energy mix in your heart, bringing you to balance. This balance grows throughout your body and aura. It helps your aura shrink to its optimal size, creating a glow about a foot around your body on all sides. Front, back, left and right sides, top and bottom. As your aura shrinks, you let go of the things hanging out in your aura that are not relevant or energy that doesn't belong to you. You are not ready for your trip into the Akashic records.

Entering Your Akashic Records

Begin this meditation with a rhythmic breathing pattern of inhaling for three counts and exhaling for three counts for at least three rounds. Then return to normal breathing. Bring your focus to your heart chakra. Relax into a room of green. In the center of that room you will see a door; there are no walls, just a door and a door jamb. Pay attention to the door. Is it utilitarian? Ornate? Sacred? Is it a curtain? This is the entrance into your Akashic records, and only you can enter here. Really, only you can see the door.

Step through the door and into your Akashic records.

Look at your feet. What do you see? Bring your eyes up slowly to take in the room. What is the room like? Is it even a room? Look around for your records Are they books? Crystals? File cabinets? Trees? Where is the light in the room coming from? Is it day or night? Your imagination is key here.

Get comfortable in your room and go explore! Remember to ask lots of questions. The Akashic records use your imagination to talk to you, and they use the language of your experiences to do it in. Yes, part of this is made up by you, until your psychic centers take over and start feeding you information from the Akasha. Don't discount what you see, but ask a lot of questions; be a bit skeptical but believe in yourself.

Exiting Your Akashic Records

When you are ready, open your eyes, step out of your records, and stamp your feet to get back into the present moment of your waking life. Know that you have access to your records anytime you wish. They are only a thought away.

As we've traveled the Akasha, we've gained confidence in what we saw and felt. We got to know our own language and reactions as we came across different things. For example, Patty learned that when her head feels like it is filled with cotton, she gets mentally tired, and when her eyes itch, it means she is in the presence of the great liar and saboteur. She knows that she needs to call in the big guns (beefy Archangel Michael) immediately before getting back to the process at hand. Jacki knows that when she is getting a trickster answer, such as, "You would never let anything like that happen, you are too powerful!" it is appealing to her ego.

We both know when we are hitting on hard truths: Jacki gets a charge up her spine; Patty gets a calm feeling and a little flip of excitement in her solar plexus. We are still learning new things about our work in the Akasha, and we continue to learn more. The Akasha is ever-changing—it's supposed to be!

You won't get it right the first time, or even the second time. Your Akashic record journey is a work in progress, and you will learn your own special techniques and build your own Akashic wisdom. We just want to share our tips and tricks to get you started.

Psychic Energy versus the Akashic Records

Right about now, especially if you are a psychic yourself, you are probably thinking: "Leading someone through the Akashic records is just performing a deep psychic reading." Oh honey, it is so much more than that! Let's break it down into the basics. When you are working with psychic energy, you are taking in someone's energy intuitively at a particular moment in time. You are intuiting what is in her aura, what is in her physical body, what is happening around her, and what the potential futures are based on all that information. The aura, or ethereal body, is filled with tons of information: hopes and dreams, discarded plans, interactions with others, responses to those interactions, fantasies, ego-driven obsessions (OMG, I have to have him!). In many ways the layers of our aura hold all the information needed to intuit answers to questions and heal ourselves.

The psychic impressions based on the collection of energy in your aura accurately portray your life and times—mostly because you put it all there, but also because it contains your history. Really good psychics tap into this level of energy and can rock your world with what they perceive there. They can get quite a bit of insight about you when they tune in to all the layers of you. Even some of your darkest secrets hang out in the ethereal body. (Oops, your astral body is showing. Here, let us tuck that in for you. Much better.)

Just like psychic readers, we learned our healing techniques by tapping into the layers of the aura, the chakras, and the Kabbalistic Tree of Life. We learned how to work with this energy to help ourselves and our clients transform and evolve spiritually. Spending lots of time surfing the aura alone taught us how to decipher the difference between what the ego wanted and what the soul wanted. We had to get really good at navigating the ethereal body and all its traps and fantasies or we wouldn't be worth a lick of salt as healers. There is great power here, but there is great deception as well; even still, never doubt that miracles happen on this psychic level.

When we accidentally stumbled (but we think our guides arranged for some calculated tripping and falling) into the Akashic records, we discovered what we thought was truly deep insight from our aura surfing was still just scratching the surface of the information available. In the Akasha we found we could take that snapshot and turn it into an epic movie with prequels just by asking, "Why?" Suddenly with each question we asked we could see the past lives that were affecting the moment and which fears were driving the bus. To our delight we found our work, magic, healing, insights, and readings were faster, clearer, and more potent when we consciously went into the Akasha, because once we were there we didn't have to plow through all the space junk that's floating in the layers of the aura.

Predictive Readings versus Akashic Readings

Who doesn't love a deck of tarot or oracle cards? About 75 percent of all tarot and oracle decks are sold for personal use, and

they're purchased almost exclusively for their predictive qualities. A funny thing happens though. As soon as the outcome
card comes into play, the negotiations begin. Ever said or heard
someone say, "*Oooo,* not liking that card. Let's see what the next
one says," "Nope, I don't want that outcome—hold on, I'm gonna
reshuffle," "Where's that damn Lovers card? I need to know I can
make her love me more," "But I *want* that job!" (Slaps down three
more cards.) Y'all are hilarious.

In the Akasha you can learn how to work with the predictions you are served up. The records will show you where you
are in your own way and how to shift your position just enough
to make an unfortunate outcome turn fortunate. When you tap
into the Akashic records while doing predictive readings, you
can tune in to the probable outcome of your future, look for the
road blocks, and then clear them. More than likely once you
clear the block, issue, or discordance, you will realize that what
you thought you wanted is no longer as desirable. What you will
end up seeing is that your most desirable outcome is the one that
aligns you with your destiny. So go ahead and use your tools—
tarot, oracle, palmistry, horoscopes, etc.—to predict where you
are going based on today's trajectory and influencing chaos, and
then change your path of destiny to suit you. That is what Jacki
and Patty call magic!

Accessing Your Akashic Records the Formal Way

If you need to be a little more formal, and ritual puts you in the
best possible space for getting into your records, we've got some
pomp and circumstance for you. We'll show you a delightful way
to prepare yourself mentally and emotionally for a visit to your
Akashic records. After you have entered the records in this fashion
a few times, your subconscious will know what to do, and it will
be easier to slip through the door in your heart chakra and enter
your record room.

Whether you choose to access your Akashic records the quick and dirty way or the formal way, you'll always need to balance your energy beforehand to prepare to enter the records.

Balancing Your Energy

Prepare for your journey by remembering your connection with the earth and the sun. Here is a great exercise to help you clear out junk in the trunk and become grounded and ready to do some exploring in your records.

Sit in a chair with your back straight and feet on the floor. Close your eyes and slowly inhale, filling your lungs. Hold your breath briefly, and then release it with a gentle exhale.

Imagine a bright light glowing above your head. Feel its warmth, and connect to the joy that is emanating from it.

With a deep breath, draw this light into the top of your head, letting it fill your crown chakra and expand it to its fullest capacity. As you exhale, feel your chakra release stress and energy that doesn't belong there.

Now shift your focus to your third eye chakra. Breathe the light into it, and watch as it expands and then releases on your exhale.

Repeat this step for each of the remaining chakras: the throat, the heart, the solar plexus, the sacral, and finally the root.

Take one last deep breath as you imagine all your chakras expanding, and exhale as you imagine all your chakras relaxing. Imagine your chakras are aligned and in balance on your pranic tube (the column of light that extends from your crown chakra to your root chakra in front of your spine).

Now, bring your attention to the ground twelve inches below your feet. This is another chakra, which we will call your earth chakra. It is round like a dinner plate and centered below your pranic tube. With a nice, deep breath send your light into your earth chakra and imagine it filling with light and expanding to thirty feet across. You may hear a hum or feel a downward tug on your energy. This is you becoming magnetized to the magnetic field of the earth, and it's a good thing. This connection is what helps you stay in your body and pull up from the earth all the energy you need to manifest your dreams and destiny.

Now imagine that you are growing roots down into the ground. Let them be thirty feet across as well, and travel to the center of the earth.

Start to feel earth energy flow through your roots into your feet. You can help this along with deep breaths and your imagination. As you are being filled with earth energy, allow it to shake loose all the energy that doesn't belong to you: other people's expectations of you, the codependent connections you've made, destructive beliefs you have about yourself. Whatever it is, let the earth energy fill you with love and cause all of the negative energy to bubble up like a shaken can of soda and pass through your aura and out into the universe. Watch as all the bubbles pop and disappear and know that you are clear.

You are now done with this grounding meditation and can begin the meditation for entering your Akashic records with the following prayer. Have fun!

Entering Your Akashic Records

Simple Meditation for Entering Your Akashic Records

First, begin by saying the prayer below.

Prayer for Entering Your Room

Great Mother, connect my heart with the heart of the earth.
Great Father, connect my heart with the heart of creation.
Fill me, balance me, and make me fully present in my body.
Guardians and guides, clear my aura of this day's travels.
    Help me release my ego and center myself within my
    divine core.
Open my psychic centers to the wisdom of my Akashic records
    and guide me through the information I uncover there.
I open my heart center, the place of Truth, to enter into my
    own Akashic records.

I call to the keepers of the Akashic records to transcend all
time and space, keeping me safe in body, mind, emotions,
and spirit.
I call to the keepers of the Akashic records to show me what I
need to know in a way that is gentle and healing.
The records are now open to me.

Next, go into your heart chakra. Imagine the door to your Akashic records. It is waiting for you to open it. Go ahead and open it and walk through.

Tarot Meditation for Initial Akashic Records Exploration

Grab your tarot deck or go online and get the images of two cards, the High Priestess and a random card (divinely guided, of course). The High Priestess is your gateway card. You will have to go through her to get into your records. The second card will frame the message you get from your guide in the record room. Let's begin.

Take three deep breaths to help you relax. Ground your energy by putting roots into the earth and sit centered on your spine. No slouching in front of the High Priestess, please. Feel free to say our suggested opening prayer on the previous page.

Focus your gaze on the High Priestess card. Take in all the details: her dress, where she's sitting, what she's holding in her hands.

Now close your eyes, picture her image, and let it come to life in your imagination.

You hear the High Priestess ask you your name and what your purpose is for going into the records.

Silently tell her your name and your purpose.

Watch as she stands and asks you to follow her.

Her throne falls away, and the two of you walk between the pillars into a long, great hallway. As you continue to walk down the hallway, a door comes into view at the end.

On the door is your full name. This is your Akashic record room.

Put your hand on the door and push it open.

The high priestess gives you a nod as you walk past her into your room.

Take a look around and note what you see . . . or don't see.

If it is dark, try turning on a light or clapping your hands. (You never know, you may have had The Clapper installed.)

Look around and see where your records are kept, what kind of seat is there for you to sit on, what your guides look like, and how many there are.

Notice the architecture, the furnishings, whether or not there is a ceiling or windows. Are there any other doors in your room? Are there people you know or who seem familiar? Are there other things besides the records? Is there any wildlife here? Is the room tidy, or is it a dump?

Now turn your attention to the place where you sit and review your records. Go and have a seat. Your guide will meet you there.

Remember the tarot card you pulled? Recall it, and it appears on the table. Watch as it comes alive, and the guide gives you a personal message for today. Thank your guide.

At this point in the meditation you can prepare to leave, you can stay and ask questions, or you can look around more.

When you are ready to leave, thank the guides and walk back toward your door. The High Priestess meets you there, and together you walk down the long corridor and back through the two columns.

As you step through the columns, you step out of the tarot card and back into your body and your daily life.

Finish by saying your closing prayer to close your records.

Exiting Your Akashic Records

Once you're ready to leave your Akashic record room, its only polite to thank your host for a lovely visit and make a graceful exit. Here is a closing prayer we use in our classes and healing sessions. It works nicely with the opening prayer and has a similar cadence.

If you choose to write your own exiting prayer, keep in mind that you want to accomplish three things: You want to be artful (poetry helps here), show gratitude, and completely close your records. This helps you come fully back to your body and your life. Having one foot in two dimensions is disorienting and will run your batteries down.

Prayer for Closing Your Akashic Records

Mother, Father, guardians, and keepers, I thank you for your guidance as I exit the Akashic records.

Spirits, masters, ancestors, I thank you and release you from today's service.

I disconnect from this reading, from any spirits, souls, entities that I may have talked about, thought about, or felt during this reading.

I ask to be put in a pillar of light to clean up any mess I may have left behind.

My Akashic records are now closed. I ask that my energy be reset and rebalanced for whatever I am about to do next.

Imagine the door in your heart closing behind you and bring your attention to your body. Put your toes in your toes and your nose in your nose. Remember where you are and who you are. If your head is spinning, take a sip of water and visualize your brilliant red root chakra sending a tap root into the earth. You may need to go hug a tree or get something to eat.

Aaaah, you've had a lovely session in the records. You've figured out some pretty interesting mysteries, and now it's time to chill. Before you celebrate with a brewski or a nap, do yourself a favor and put some notes down in your Akashic visits journal. We suggest you write down anything that happened that you didn't fully understand. With each visit, these mysteries will work themselves out and make more sense. We have often gotten messages that come in layers, and it can oftentimes take several visits to get the whole picture.

Keeping an Akashic journal is like keeping a dream journal or looking at clouds. You will be interpreting what you see and feel. Use whatever way works best for you—writing, drawing, making collages. Also, having a running documentary of your journeys will be priceless as you look back and see how far you've come. Doing this in a fairly organized way will help you see that your path of enlightenment is actually going somewhere.

Chapter 6

Resistance to Accessing Your Akashic Records

In every class we teach there is at least one person who says they can't see anything when they go into their record room. During one convention, there was a gentleman who took all three classes, and in each one he pointed out that he didn't get anything on any of the meditations or visualizations. Really, he was the only one who didn't get anything and was very vocal about it. By the time the third class came about Jacki had lost it. She started to say, "There is something wrong with you!" but she pulled back at the last second and instead said, "There is something we need to discuss after class to lift your block." We dedicate this chapter to this man, our resistant visualizer, and hope this makes amends for Jacki's lack of patience in that one class.

When we took our student aside to see where his block might be, we learned that he is a tarot reader. When we asked him how he receives information in his tarot readings, he said it just comes and that he takes clues from the images on the cards. I asked him if he ever got information without the cards, and he hesitated before admitting that he does. Why would the Akashic records work any differently? The Akasha is there all the time; you are the variable. You will see them and interact with them in the way that you are most familiar with. From this base your practice and develop your technique.

Our reluctant student taught us how to help others move past the resistance to connecting with their records. We have found that the people who have a hard time "seeing" their records are all expecting to see a movie, images on an oracle deck, or a spiritual realm like the ghost whisperer does. When we ask a roomful of students how many people see the psychic realm like the ghost whisperer, there is always one person who raises their hand. Jacki then calls them out—"You are an anomaly!"—to help release the rest of the students' expectations of perfection. Ninety percent of us won't see the spiritual realm as clearly as the ghost whisperer does right out of the gate. We will struggle for impressions, squint our eyes, put pressure on our third eye, and generally try too hard. Can you imagine if you were able to see the other realms like you see this one all the time? It would be brain-melting—or brain-breaking at the very least.

✒Akashic Tales from Aunt Jacki

When I first began reading and working as a psychic, I really felt the tools were doing most of the work—and they probably were. I was not a "natural born" psychic who could pull answers out of thin air, and for a long while I felt that I was inadequate and not worthy of working psychically. That is, until I realized that the gifts I was developing in myself were actually more controlled and connected with who I am as a person than if I had been born seeing spirits and grew up being bombarded with psychic impressions.

Now, twenty-five years later, I have seen many natural born psychics burn themselves out and struggle to find control. I am now teaching them how to turn it off or slow the input; just like I teach you how to increase the input.

Don't discount yourself just because you weren't "born this way." Keep asking questions of spiritual advisers whom you admire. Take their classes.

When we ask our "ghost whisperers" how they see the information or the spirit, every time they have said that they start with a feeling or understanding and then the form takes shape for them. This is reassuring; they're going through the same process as the rest of us—it just happens quicker for them than it does for you; they are naturals and you are in training. Neither is better, just different.

Is It Real or Is It My Imagination?

Akashic wisdom talks to you through your imagination and uses the language of your experience to paint the picture.

Think about that. Your own wisdom is created as you build upon an idea. You learn to count before you learn the shapes of the numbers. Once you learn your numbers, you move to simple addition and subtraction. Once you master that, the teacher shows you that $2 + 2 + 2 + 2 = 8$ or $2 \times 4 = 8$, and a whole new world opens up to you. The Akashic records work the same way: your experiences are the language and your imagination is where the information comes through. Even whisperers use their imagination to interpret the energy that they are translating. Get several mediums in the room, and while they will probably all pick up on the same information, each person will have a different perspective and interpretation of what the information means.

The answer to your question is yes, it is your imagination. Your imagination is that innocent trust needed to accept the wisdom that is moving through you; you may start with your imagination, but you are not making it all up. Merriam-Webster defines imagination as "the act or power of forming a mental image of something not present to the senses or never before wholly perceived in reality." You are finding new information every time you access your Akashic records, so there will always be something "never before wholly perceived in reality." The trick is not to judge where the initial images are coming from, especially when you are working from a place of spiritual peace and insight. In essence you're co-creating the image in your mind's eye (imagination) with the wisdom from the Akasha. Your guides are merging the memories of your current experiences and knowledge with new spiritual ideas to inspire you to think a new thought. It can feel quite magical and very much like you're making it all up, sorta. Isn't that fun?

Your experiences are what your wisdom is made of. Just as Jesus tapped into the stories, experiences, and lessons he learned from others to interpret the lessons of the Divine, divine helpers in the Akashic records will at times send you information to prepare you for your next Akashic session. Really, it's true.

✒Akashic Lessons from Aunt Jacki

I often find that when I am reading or healing for others with the Akashic records there is usually some recent experience or new piece of wisdom that applies to our session. One day I got into a conversation about angels and learned about one I had not heard of before (Archangel Haniel). My next reading came in, and during our session that new angel kept coming to mind. I stopped and asked my client if she had ever heard of this angel, and if she had, if he was relevant to her situation. My client was shocked because she was just reading about that angel the day before and had felt a connection. There was the confirmation she needed, and I had a new experience.

Akashic Lessons from Aunt Patty

For a long time I was helping a client learn her value as a peaceful presence in the world. Though she wanted to stop dealing with "evil" in combative ways, she was pretty resistant to this idea. She was a warrior, after all. I learned a lot from her journey, and this was very timely, because after we started working together I began to collect other peaceful warriors as clients. Each and every one of them was learning a new way to be an agent of God that did not include swords, shields, armor, or gory battles. Their level of powerlessness, grief, exhaustion, and deep abandonment was making them not want to be here. It was difficult for them to face pain and not fight it with might. This made them feel like their life was pointless, and often depression and physical illness ensued. I was able to tap into the Akashic wisdom around this issue and guide these lovely, gentle people onto their new path of being the light instead of fighting for the light.

Yes, we looked at many, many historical stories about personal sacrifices and martyrdom, and each and every one helped them heal their wounds and come to terms with who they were, so they could choose to embrace who they are trying to become.

The moral of the story is that fantastical past life memories are not always wishful thinking of a timid person fantasizing about being Buffy the vampire slayer. They can be memories to help us change our perception of ourselves for the better.

Memories . . . Light the Corners of the Akasha!

Asking questions can help you better see and understand your Akashic records, and sometimes it takes practice to get the questions just right. Asking questions like, "What is next?" or "Where does that lead?" or our favorite, "What does that mean?" are all good starting points. Try tugging on words to see where they take you.

Tugging on a word to paint a new picture is very akin to bringing up a memory from childhood. A happy birthday party, a particularly vivid Christmas morning, or your favorite bedroom as a child—while those long-tucked-away memories may be unnecessary to today's life, they made a big impact on your young mind. When you practice bringing up a memory with specific questions, you will really embrace that memory.

We do an exercise in class where we ask one person to describe their childhood bedroom while everyone else tunes in. When we are about halfway through the description, we ask some people to tell the group other things they see in the speaker's bedroom to see if they are right. Many times the class reminds the speaker of things they forgot about, like the sports equipment in the corner, or their bad habit of hiding dishes under the bed, or that the cat loved to sleep on their pillow.

You will have to do this exercise on your own, but the feeling of pulling up this memory is exactly like pulling up Akashic memories.

Visualization Exercise: Your Childhood Bedroom

Relax and take a couple of deep breaths. You are going to do some happy remembering here, so get mellow and enjoy the journey.

Call up a memory of your favorite childhood room. What did the door into your room look like? Was it at the end of the hall? At the top of the stairs? Off the kitchen? What did you have to pass to get to your room? Did you share your room with anyone?

When you open the door to you room, was it quiet or did it squeak? Did you have carpeting in your room? What color was the floor?

When you walked into the room, what was right in front of you? Were there any awards on the wall or shelves? Were your toys splayed out everywhere or were they put away?

What was to the right and left? Where was the closet? How many windows were in the room? What color were the walls?

What kind of bed did you have? Did you have a dresser? What was your favorite thing in the room?

Was your room messy or clean? How did this room make you feel? What was your favorite memory here?

Let yourself be in the room and remember for a while; let the story of this point in your childhood form and flesh out.

Question Trumps Resistance Every Time!

Asking questions while in your Akashic records breaks through your resistance on every level. When you ask yourself a question, you always answer yourself (especially when you talk out loud to yourself). When you give yourself a blank stare, that means you do not believe yourself, so ask the question in a slightly different way. We find that asking "Where am I?" is a very powerful question and a great place to start. If you are giving yourself the silent treatment with that question, ask something with a yes or no answer: "Am I in my Akashic records?", "Am I looking at my own life?", "Am I looking at a past life?" Let yourself use questions to drill down to the details. Start with the big picture and then get more specific as you go on. For example, when you are first approaching the door to your Akashic records:

* Q: Is it a door, curtain, window, or portal?
* A: Door.

* Q: **What does the door look like? Is it functional or ornate? Is it wood or a curtain? Is it square or curved at the top?**
* A: It is a functional door, like my office door, and it has a window in it.
* Q: **After you open the door, what do you see? Is it a room, a garden, a library, a cave?**
* A: A library.
* Q: **What book is open on the table for you to see? Is it a children's book? An encyclopedia? A novel? A history book?**
* A: It's a biography—mine!
* Q: **Which story of your life is it open to? Childhood? Past Life? Young Adult?**
* A: It's open to the story of my life today.
* Q: **What is it trying to tell you? Is there anything else in the room to give you a clue?**
* A: I see piles of brand-new money with the bands still around the bills. But all the money is under locked glass. There are at least four locked glass domes with money in them. It is so frustrating.

When you put all the pieces together, you can see a bigger story and then dig further into healing and even doing a little Akashic record magic.

Remember that resistance is best addressed with a gentle touch. When you try and bat down your resistance with pressure or expectation, your resistance just gets worse. What resists persists, so if you resist being resistant, you will be left with resistance. But when you coax it out with a trail of gentle questions, you will open up more fully to the experience.

Chapter 7

Everything Leads Up to Now—
You Are Eternal but Never Old

What is going on today started a long, long time ago so it's OK if it takes a few sessions (or twelve) to sort through it.

When you decide you want to improve your life in some way, heal an issue, or change a habit, it doesn't happen in a snap. We all want the magic pills to cure our spiritual ills, but the journey is essential to really change your outcome. Even smokers who quit "cold turkey" have withdrawals and moments of weakness. They get crabby at times, but hold on to the belief that not smoking is more important than smoking. From the outside it may seem like they're having an easy time of it (bless their hearts), but they're going on more of an internal journey than an external one. Every change in your life requires a shift in perception. That shift takes patience and courage to keep looking for more triggers that could stop your spiritual evolution.

Everything in your life (and lifetimes) leads up to now . . . this moment, right here. At times you have thrived. At times you have muddled on through just to get to the other side of a creek of crap. At times you were phoning it in and not making any great strides in life. Each experience builds upon the last and makes you who you are today. Contrary to the messages your fears are telling you, the person your experiences have made you become is an amazing one. Your Akashic records hold all of those experiences for you, waiting for you to uncover them, review them, and decide how they will work for you (or not). Getting started on this path is as simple as stepping upon it, honoring yourself, and being willing to dig deep.

🖋 Lessons from Aunt Jacki

There is a Hindu prayer that I keep in my office. To me this prayer is for my body and all the experiences my spirit has had with it. I not only feed my body with food, but I feed my spirit with people, words, fears, limitations, love, acceptance, ego. . . . My spiritual body is made up of all of the emotions and experiences it is fed. It is my spiritual body, in alignment with the mental, emotional, and physical bodies, that makes up my everyday reality, and proves my deep inner beliefs I didn't even know I have (tricky bastards!).

When I stop for a moment, tune in to where I am today, and give myself some love and acceptance, I can start to make a change. The last three lines of this prayer never fail to inspire me. Since that is all I have memorized, I repeat the ending of the prayer to myself when I am overly stressed and need to get back into the now.

Your homework, before you finish reading this section, is to read the prayer, get misty, hug yourself, copy the prayer down, and keep it handy.

Hindu Prayer for the Body
(author unknown)

I recognize you are the temple
in which my spirit and creative energy dwell.
I have created you from my need
to have my spirit manifested on earth
so that I may have this time to learn and grow.
I offer you this food so that you may continue

to sustain my creative energy, my spirit, my soul.
I offer this food to you with love,
and a sincere desire for you to remain free
from disease and disharmony.
I accept you as my own creation.
I need you.
I love you.

You may have to visit a particular issue over and over again in order to peel away the layers of experiences and beliefs that hold a harmful issue in place. It's OK, you've worked all your life (or lifetimes) to get it here, perfectly snug, hiding within all of your positive experiences, and it may take a minute to clear it out.

Akashic record work gives you insight into yourself and the key to building your own personal wisdom. If everything was easy, we would never need to be wise. (Think of it this way: A lack of wisdom can quickly lead to boredom. Boredom leads to trouble. Trouble leads to experience. And experience finally leads to wisdom. You can't avoid it.) In this book we're happy to increase your wisdom on this subject by giving you lots and lots to think about and experience!

Your journey is unique to you. All we can do is set up the basics; you take it from there. Be kind to yourself on this journey, and don't expect to master it your first time in. (Are you seeing the "wash, rinse, repeat" theme here?) This is an exploration of your spirit, psyche, and everything that makes you tick. You are a miracle of coping mechanisms, complexes, and spiritual back-up systems that keep you slightly sane. Thank yourself for everything you've done to keep putting one proverbial foot in front of the other through all these lifetimes, and then get excited—because now you have a new box of tools to make the journey better and more rewarding.

Start Your Akashic Journey by Honoring Yourself

No matter how you feel about your life, or about yourself, the best way for you to launch your healing journey in the Akashic records is by celebrating you. This is more easily said than done for many of us, as we have been trained to always put ourselves last, trust ourselves last, not be too greedy, and never ask for anything. For those of you who have already mastered this process, carry on with the good work, Oh, and since we have never met a spiritual student who has mastered this completely, if you have, please drop us a line—we would love to meet you. We've got questions.

Think about it. As children we start out as the center of the universe, and the first big lesson we have to learn is how to become part of the bigger world. We are taught to take turns, be gentle with other children's feelings, not run with scissors, wash our hands, and not break the crayons because other kids may want to use them. We learn the pecking order in grade school and battle with self-esteem in high school. Then we are launched into adulthood and realize that we are accountable to even more people and the world is *huge* and kinda scary when your paycheck is less than your bills. *Fail! Fail! Fail!* is what life can start to feel like.

Well, congratulations! You failed, and that is more valuable than always succeeding. We learn more from our failures than our successes. Really, your successes are born out of the lessons you've learned from your failures. When you learn to play an instrument, or a sport, or color a picture, you first learn how to be terrible at it before you can master it. Why would the rest of your life be any different?

Embracing failure is a difficult concept, as we culturally value the easily successful and the miracle endings. We elevate the virtuosos of the world, the natural born talent, the get-rich-quick schemes. It's time to change that reality.

Truth be told, it's more in your nature to value the things you have to work hard for. When you power through and stick to something, you gain an expertise and skill that only you can learn through overcoming challenges and fixing broken toys. So why do you try to create the shortcut when you know you'll feel like you've cheated yourself of a delicious win? This dichotomy of beliefs creates the struggle where we no longer know how to honor and celebrate ourselves. We are constantly invalidating ourselves with "I can't," and this keeps us off balance. It's time to shock yourself back into place with a celebration of you—your flaws as well as your successes!

We may even be so bold as to suggest throwing yourself a party when you get into your record room. (Bumpy cake, yay!) Deciding to work in your records with honor and respect in order to fix or upgrade all aspects of yourself is like hitting a grand slam that wins the World Series. So pop open the champagne, and let it shower you with love as you revel in just how amazing you are. We don't give you accolades lightly. We know about you . . . you have been places and have done things that have moved the universe forward. You are an important piece of our fabulous world, so thanks for hanging in there.

Getting Around the Self-Tricks

Overcoming Self-Doubt

One of the more challenging things you are going to face when it comes to self-help is believing in yourself. Doubt in yourself and your process is one of the first ways you will trick yourself out of making the changes you desire. How many times have you talked yourself out of a compliment? That is the baby version of what we see happen all the time with our clients.

Embrace your strengths and wisdom when it is time to heal, and believe that you are worthy of love, success, and forgiveness. Keep that in mind when you go into your records with the plea in your voice to heal you, teach you how to make money, release you from your addiction, or bring you the love you long for. Without the conviction that you are repairable, it's very challenging to heal yourself. With that said, you can get a lot done before you take your Akashic record journal to a professional.

Telling Yourself the Truth

Another way you can trick yourself out of truth and potential healing is to justify yourself through the filter called ego. One of the important jobs of the ego is to keep you alive. It does this by making sure you avoid pain, since pain is often the precursor to death. Avoiding pain is always a good thing in ego's book, and the issue becomes flattened into an all or nothing, black-and-white kind of thing. Pain equals bad.

But not all pain is life-threatening—in fact, a lot of it isn't. It's the shades of gray about pain that help you grow. Pain can motivate you to move, mature, and evolve, especially when you're dealing with emotional and mental pain. Some pain can actually be good for you. It gets you off the proverbial couch of your life and back in the game.

Maybe you agree with us that pain is complex, and we could stand to learn something from it. So how can we get around the ego, which can only tell us what is most important to our survival, a.k.a., pain avoidance? Fortunately, we have other ways to get at the truth.

Picture this: You are in the records, and you have a goal in mind as you ask your big question. Typically you will stand there as you await your answer, and when it arrives, you will allow it to slowly sink in. And then, wait for it . . . and then you hedge. "Was that my guide, or my imagination, or wishful thinking" (code words for ego)? We can hear the wheels turning from over here. This is where you trick yourself with wacked out answers from your personal agenda (also code for ego). When thoughts start rolling around in your head and go through several incarnations of the "right" answer, you know you've lost a grip on the truth. Every time you doubt, negotiate, rewrite, justify, and fuss about the "guidance," realize that your ego has taken control.

Higher truth is felt in a totally different part of your body and gives you a completely different experience. Truth hits you in the gut. You'll get a flip flop or buzzy sensation that blossoms upward to your heart. It fills you with a calm knowing, and it's impossible to doubt it; you just can't feel any doubt anywhere—not even in your head, because your head is not in this game. You are able to quickly move into acceptance and know that the decision made is final, at least for now, and staying focused on the here and now becomes really easy. Now you can act on the guidance because it's real and it came from your higher self/God/your guides, and you know it.

When in doubt, imagine you have your own personal Truth Meter. Picture a meter with a needle that swings from left to right on a scale from one to ten, with one being a lie and ten being the truth. The next time you make a statement, a confession, or tell a story, watch the meter's needle. If it lands on a one or two, I suggest you rephrase your statement or question the validity of that belief. Part of your empowerment is to learn to not lie to yourself.

Leggo My Ego

The ego, not to be confused with the aura, is a very powerful force and can trick you into buying its bill of goods. Your ego can not only convince you that the sky is green and the grass is blue, it can convince you that you're the genius who made it that way. Clever little ego also places lots of things in your aura to ensure its agenda is followed, keeping it king of (your) castle. Viewing the ego through the wisdom of the Akasha helps you bypass that all-powerful wizard of an ego and see it for the little imp behind the curtain it really is. This sure puts things in a perspective that is much more manageable and, may we add, realistic.

✒ Aunt Jacki's Life Lessons

In my early days as a reader, it was easy to get lost in my client's ego, especially when the client was mentally damaged and living in a fantasy world or when they wanted something so badly it colored all other important divine information. Then there is the astral realm too, which talks so loudly it can be difficult to distinguish what is information for my client and what is background noise. Now that I can access the Akashic records, readings are a breeze. My clients aren't always a breeze, but I can get around that with much less struggle now.

Healer! Heal Thyself!

You are your best healer. Actually, you are the one who does all the healing work, so you are your *only* healer; everyone else is just a facilitator of your process. To some of you this is old news, but most travelers on the healing path wait for a teacher, master, shaman, or guru to do any healing work. To be honest, that is where we both began until we were strapped for cash and our scrapper attitudes came out and said, "Let me take a stab at this myself—what can it hurt?"

*

Once you begin this journey, you are going to find many opportunities throughout your day to dip into your Akashic records and do a little healing. Don't get all OCD on us, though—the middle of a board meeting may not be an opportune time to tune out the world. When you find something, take note and work on it later. If it's really a bad moment, excuse yourself to the lavatory. You are almost guaranteed privacy there to take a moment and work out your spiritual emergency.

The best thing you can do for yourself on your Akashic journey is to consciously keep yourself in balance. You can do this by:

1. Rejuvenating your body, mind, and heart with joyful experiences—ya know, keep it light. There will be enough challenges to your joy with the heavy things you will find and heal in your Akashic records. Make sure you counterbalance those sessions with play, fun, and creative activities and being silly.

2. Resting after a healing. Going to work after clearing a demon from your beliefs can be too much of a juxtaposition. Having to herd children and make dinner after reclaiming a past life can feel a little raw. Plan your healing sessions accordingly and get rest afterward. Sleep is a necessary component to integrate your healing session fully into your life. Also, rest between sessions. Doing this work for yourself every day, several times a week can be too much. Time itself is the master healer and integrator for all of your new wisdom.

3. Drinking, eating, and being merry . . . in balance. We are not dietitians, nor are we sweating with the oldies, but in our experience when we eat and drink too much crap food the healing work is more difficult. There are enough studies confirming the correlation between eating, stress, and spiritual contentedness to say that there is something to this.

4. Finding the love in everything, and it will be reflected in you. Start your day with inspirational, positive words;

contemplate the meaning of those words in your life and then you will find that you'll have a much more loving day than not. Call it "spending time with the light" and you will glow all day.

As much as we want a miracle to save us from our own folly, the healing journey is just that—a journey. It's not a teleport to the end of the race. When we try to shortcut the journey, we are sent back to the beginning to start over again, only this time with feeling, personal truth, and an ego that we distract with a new set of crayons.

Even if you feel you have completely messed up your life irrevocably, you have not. Healing yourself by slowly peeling away the layers you find in your Akashic records gives you that second, third, and 120th chance that you may need. It's not the one-time healing that makes the most profound effect; it's the healing that finally gets to the core of the matter and changes the way you address life.

As you play and heal in the Akasha, remember to celebrate your wins, get around your own tricks, and watch out for that ego of yours who can try and run the show. This is your own unique journey, so be kind to yourself, be courageous, and above all, be tenacious!

Chapter 8

Helpers and Divine Beings

OK, how many of you can see your jazz clearly, without prejudice or bias? . . . Hmmm, not too many hands in the air. It's OK, we can't either. That's why we have guides and healers in our life. We all need assistance seeing the truth when it comes to our own stories. It provides us with a checks and balances system that consists of honest, intelligent people who keep us from tricking ourselves right out of being responsible for our screw-ups. When you start believing your own press, it's time to get an impartial, unbiased, truth seeker.

Having spiritual backup is imperative to real healing. There is no point in going into your Akashic records and doing a tap dance around the truth. You won't learn your lesson, and your feet will get blisters. Go for the brass ring of enlightenment and get a healing team together that's got your back when you don't.

The records were designed to specifically retain information: historical facts, our thoughts, emotions, and dreams. They also contain echoes of each potential that is possible from each decision and experience we have or don't have. This is why we need guides to help us. Without them we could become very lost and confused by what we are seeing. Also the dimension of the Akasha does not play by the same rules as the dimension that we live in. It can't, because it serves a very different purpose, and linear thinking is too limiting for what the Akasha is designed to do. Our guides help translate the Akashic energy into our language so we can make good use of it for our own growth.

Your guides and divine allies know their way around all levels of the Akasha; it is their playground! They not only bring inspiration, divine energy, and celebration, they will also help you get through your own doubts, filters, lies, and sabotage. You'll feel like finding and addressing what needs to be healed is the hardest part, but frankly it's what you're here to do. This part of the journey is the crux of why your records are important. When you drill down through those fears, blocks, and issues, you find the truth—that you are healing. With each layer you uncover you will learn about that special way you hid yourself from the world and from yourself. This is called revealing your light. Once you find that little gem of information, the guides will help you figure out how to dismantle the issue and come back to the real you.

Choosing Your Healing Team: Akashic Records Meet and Greet

We suggest you get folks from both sides of the veil to help you on your search for truth. We all need a village and a boatload of validation to help raise us up when we're unsure of ourselves while dealing with our challenges. When assembling your perfect village of healers please remember that you are a precious commodity. Your guides must be agenda-free, compassionate, respectful, and most of all non-judgmental. If you don't feel safe sharing your story about the choices you've made and the feelings you have with your guide, say good-bye and find another.

On This Side of the Veil

Find a trusted therapist, counselor, spiritual healer, or Reiki practitioner. Since this kind of work is filled with metaphors and reflecting on past experiences, you will want allies who are intuitive, good with dream interpretation, and who understand human psychology.

While we have worked on each other in the past, we have also worked with other healers, too—and not all of them are on the same Akashic path we are. What we found with our healing partners is that we can explore new ideas, learn new techniques, and gain new perspectives with deeper insight for ourselves.

✒ If We Can Do It, So Can You

Even though we are sisters, when we started to work together we didn't know a lot about each other, as there is a nine-year difference between us. (We won't tell you who is older.) Honestly, it was very difficult to share some of our inner working with each other. Sometimes you don't want your sister to know your sins, and telling your woes to a stranger feels easier. We did it though; we learned about each other, and let the Akashic records teach us that there is no judgment in healing, only events and responses.

A good healing partner will help you find the exact question that will lead you to your own answer. Their job is to encourage and push you along your path, but they can't find the answers for you. If your partner tells you an insight about you, it is easy to take it personally and dismiss it as their opinion. But when you uncover a truth on your own, you will remember and you will own it.

On the Other Side of the Veil

As for your helpers on the other side of the veil, you will do best if you start with your guardian angel, higher self, and the guides in the Akashic records, which are described later in this chapter. The more you work in the records, the more guides will come to help you, bringing their expertise along with them.

Any healing ally needs to get to know you (and you them), and a relationship needs to be built before you can really trust what you are experiencing with them. The same goes for your spiritual allies. You need to recognize their voice or energy, not only in the Akashic records but outside of them too. Building a relationship with your allies is not restricted to your Akashic record room; you will find them talking to you throughout your day.

Ask spirit allies to show you how to recognize them. Ask them to send you a sign in your waking world. Jacki used to get feathers in her path when her guides were confirming what she was working on. Now she recognizes the energy shift in her life when it's a message and when it is a random happening. Patty sees the numbers seven and eleven together often. She knows now that it's not a message to grab a coffee or a Big Gulp on the way to work, but it's a "Hello Patty, yes you are doing great!" Building a spiritual relationship with your healing team is rewarding and goes beyond the Akashic record room.

The guides you will work with most often will be the ones who have a warmer, friendly approach (let's face it, we are more willing to work with the friendly ones, too). These are your Akashic teachers and healers. They will be there to talk to you, answer questions, and inspire you to try a new perspective.

You can count on your guides to be patient; they will make a point several different ways until you understand what they're trying to teach you. You will be shown multiple sides of the story, given possible outcomes based on your choices, and asked great leading questions to get you off that one-dimensional thinking you are so fond of. They will do all this by drawing on your own pop culture references, memories, and education and experience. We hope you like solving mysteries and roleplaying, because you may end up in your record room dressed up as Dorothy with a Scarecrow, Tin Man, and Lion with you on a yellow brick road on the way to see the wizard. If that happens, know that you are in for a grand lesson.

The keepers and divine beings that show up to assist you will be unique to each and every one of you, but we'll present the ones we work with regularly and give you some suggestions about how to make the most of their expertise. Building relationships with your own guides is welcomed and encouraged, but if you get stuck, call on ours. They are universal and the whiz kids of the Akashic records.

Here's our who's who list of the Akashic guides.

The Earthly Beings

Greeters

It's always nice to have a cheerleader and a witness on our adventures, and your greeters fill this role nicely. Greeters tend to be the first wave of guides you meet and are often your silent partners once the work begins. They help you feel welcome, loved, and confident that you are in the right place. They will comfort you when you are distressed and flood you with love and acceptance constantly. They are most often called loved ones and ancestors because that's exactly who they are: people who have an affinity to you and want you to succeed. You can consider them members of your soul family because they probably have incarnated with you many times and you share a common goal: the advancement of your soul. They are as dedicated to your evolution as you are to theirs. When it's their turn to incarnate, you will probably be one of their guides (provided you graduate from guide school).

Loved Ones

Loved ones are often members of your human family and have been your siblings, parents, aunts and uncles, grandparents, and even great grandparents. Of course they have crossed over to the other side, but they have proven they can guide you with open honesty, love you unconditionally, and joyfully help you on your spiritual path. Other loved ones can include a best friend, a favorite teacher, or someone you respected greatly while they were alive. These handpicked loved ones will be there for you every step of the way in your Akashic journeys.

Ancestors

Loved ones who are three or four generations removed are referred to as ancestors. Not just anyone gets to be an ancestor who guides you in your Akashic records. They have to prove that they are able to be supportive, practically agenda-free, and have learned their lessons. Having ancestors as guides will come in handy when it's time to look at issues coming down from the family tree.

The Divine Beings

Divine beings exist in the Akashic records already and have been there all along. This is their hangout, and from the work we have been doing, we have discovered that they connect to our lives through the Akashic records. How divine, and what a relief! You never have to navigate your records on your own, and you were never meant to. There will always be guides and teachers in your records for you to interact with. Much of the time they will be hidden, but you will always be aware of their presence. Like all good teachers, they are there to make sure you learn your lessons and catch you if you start to really screw up. Many who work with the records say they experience a hierarchy of spiritual beings that have their own job and expertise.

Record Keepers

Ladies and Gentlemen, the Chairman of the Board . . . The bigwigs in the Akashic realm are the record keepers, and they do not come out of the stacks very often. They are in charge of the flow and integrity of information given. These noble guides aren't so concerned with your personal processes, but rest assured that they truly care about you. The Akashic record keepers express this cool persona and hang back in the stacks for a good reason: they need to monitor all that is happening in the records and be ready to act when they need to. It's that detached, objective observer role that makes them come off as a team of Spock clones. Still, they answer to a higher authority, and are not your personal librarians, so show them respect.

The keepers, as we like to call them, are there to guard you and your records from harm, both intentional and unintentional. They keep other people from mucking around in your room and stop you from doing any real damage to yourself. Yes, we do need protection, even from ourselves. They are guardians of all Akashic records, and they take their job very seriously.

When it's time to make some changes, the record keepers determine your readiness and capacity to move to a broader wavelength of information. They are responsible for giving you the bigger picture, and they do this by narrowing the field for you, only giving the exact perfect information to you as you need it. No distractions, and no *"Oooo,* look . . . . shiny." Please don't feel controlled or edited by them; they are committed to your evolution. They are not babysitters, nor are they pushovers. If what you need to see makes you feel a tad squeamish, they are patient while the next hierarchies of guides help you accept the truth. Everyone has Akashic record keepers, and they do the record changing while you do the requesting of said changes, and never the other way around.

Masters

The next tier of guides are the master teachers or master healers. The masters are the beings who help you understand what's going on and are always available for a chat. They are responsible for translating messages, untangling your confusion with helpful hints and metaphors, and asking you probing questions to get you back on track.

These guides are very wise, but don't treat them like encyclopedias; they make you work for your wisdom, because they know it's in your searching and puzzling that you will begin to understand. They know you personally and intimately and know why you are there even when you are not sure. They help you discover what the real issues are, and they do their best to help you dissolve the illusions so you can see the truth.

As soon as you're ready to get down to healing, the master teacher becomes a master healer in a blink of an eye, and executes the transformational protocol needed. The master healer will help you rewrite or break agreements, remove toxic energy, and heal your wounds. We'll go over all of that in the next chapters.

For fun and to help you understand them better, the masters will show themselves as goddesses, ascended masters, archangels, lightworkers, and even other, non-divine beings (such as archetypes, characters from the tarot, and pop culture). We often see Kwan Yin, Brigid, Archangel Michael, Buddha, the Dark Man, and even the Wizard of Oz (seriously). At times you may not see anyone but get a feeling that someone is there, especially when you start picking up on a disembodied voice (that's always fun).

The Goddesses We Adore

Brigid

A Celtic goddess who has stood the test of time! We call upon Brigid when our emotional, mental, and spiritual toxicity has overwhelmed us. It can feel so much like a regular viral infection with body aches, lethargy, and the whole nine yards that we call it the woo woo flu. Whether it's the woo woo flu or other kinds of toxins (negatively charged energy) in your aura, Brigid will literally walk through you and pull all that nasty energy off. She will also take on the hooks and drains (see chapter 11) that are plaguing you so you can clear them without drama. Brigid is Celtic warrior, but she is also the keeper of the hearth, a midwife, a bard, and she is known for her healing wells—she even provided a well of healing waters for you in your record room. Brigid is brave and compassionate and protective of all her kin, which is basically everyone. She reminds us of the Archangel Khamael.

Soul Parts

We have a concept to throw at you, so get ready. Sometimes we need to move pieces of our soul around in case something breaks and we need replacement parts. We are talking about the idea that not all of our soul incarnates in one lifetime. Our gigantic soul invests only a part of itself in each incarnation (we discuss soul parts more in chapter 9). There are several reasons for this, but what we have come to know is that if we screw up and go into that dark place and don't want to live, a part of our soul can embody that "beyond repair" status and hold it away from the rest of the incarnating soul and give it a chance to complete its life experience. It's a phenomenal, fail-safe plan that often works. Conversely, we have to have some soul in reserve to replace that broken part. Hence, replacement parts! Very efficient and very cool.

Kwan Yin

Kwan Yin is the Buddhist goddess of compassion and mercy. When you have wounded soul parts that need healing, Kwan Yin is the goddess to call upon. She will help you heal the past and guide lost soul parts to make sure everyone is where they belong. The legend of Kwan Yin is that in her deep compassion for humanity she decided not to return to God until all souls have returned. When you decide to heal your wounded soul parts instead of ignore them, you are helping Kwan Yin with her mission.

Lilith

Babylonian goddess of night, Adam's first wife in Jewish mythology, and patron goddess of women and children, Lilith can help when we are dealing with any kind of abuse. When we come across young, wounded soul parts or inner children who have suffered abuse, Lilith will help them feel validated and venerate their sacrifice. Lilith will be there to exact justice and help them feel whole again. You can call upon Lilith to help you overcome the pain of your abuse no matter if it's from this lifetime or another.

✒ How Jacki Started Working with Lilith

While working with a client on releasing blocks to her health, we came upon soul parts from her childhood abuser. We discovered that during the abuse, the abuser had taken some of my client's soul parts and left their own to be able to continue feeding off her divine energy. As my client worked on healing, the abuser was fed even more. When my client and I discovered this, she was pissed and wasn't willing to let go of the abuser's soul parts so they could be healed! She felt that would be absolution for her abuser, and she wanted retribution! During my client's tirade, Lilith stepped forward to help. My client's soul parts were returned healed and empowered by Lilith, while the abuser's soul parts were taken away to be dealt with by divine judgment.

My client felt as if this person would face some kind of judgment for what they did to her as a child, and she was able to let it go. Sometimes we need the mama bear to fight for us, and Lilith will certainly do that.

Kali

Known as the Destroyer, the ender of cycles, and the bringer of transformation and change, Hindu goddess Kali is not to be messed with. She is exacting in her work, and she enjoys the very tough jobs. Call upon her when you have a bond, contract, or energy block that is resistant to everything. Her cache is rich with every type of weapon known to man, and she has six arms and knows how to use them.

How Patty Works with Kali

Anytime I find an energy pattern that looks like wound-up wire or a corkscrew, I call upon Kali to help me out. The fact that it's made of metal tells me that this energy is really locked down. Usually my client has been in a very weak place and someone has taken complete advantage of that and locked him into an oppressive agreement. Once my client and I can identify how this happened (his state of mind or reason for weakness), I call upon Kali to bust the agreement. I've seen Kali show up with a chainsaw, dynamite, and a jackhammer before, so she has definitely embraced power tools. After Kali's destruction it's much easier for my client to reclaim his power and self-esteem.

Ascended Masters

Jesus the Christ

Jesus is the right hand of God and the historical figure known as Jesus of Nazareth whose life inspired Christianity. In the records, we work with the Christ energy more than his persona to help us make sweeping changes in our beliefs, however they are manifesting. The Christ energy is about unconditional love, innocence, and tolerance. You can ask Jesus the Christ to help you with any kind of healing or advice, though we often see him volunteering to help remove pain bodies in the healing waters (see page 212), as he has mad transformational skills.

Jesus lived his life as an example to us of what embodying the Christ energy can look like. Buddha, Mary, Mohammad, and Kwan Yin, to name the few, also embodied that energy. If you have been hurt, angered, or have suffered persecution for being Christian or by Christian dogma, Jesus the Christ can and will help you heal. Remember, Jesus of Nazareth was not a Christian and can show you another perspective on his life and teaching. So don't be shy— he's amazing, has a great sense of humor, and knows everything. All he needs is your invitation.

Siddhartha Gautama the Buddha

The master of compassion and taking the middle path, this Buddha teaches us the necessity and wisdom in releasing limiting beliefs and reminds us to live moderately—not in extremes. Siddhartha was born a wealthy prince in the sixth century but rejected this life to learn how to relieve deep poverty in his father's kingdom. He studied with aesthetic monks and denied himself earthly pleasures and necessities while spending many years seeking enlightenment through meditation. His own enlightenment came when he discovered the wisdom in living life in balance, which he later taught as taking the middle path. In our Akashic healings, Buddha always steps up to the plate to heal us when our excesses have made us to toxic and support us with dreams filled with teachings as we embrace new spiritual habits.

Mary, Mother of God

When we talk about Mary, we are referring to the historical figure known as the mother of Jesus. She's a compassionate healer and mother to us all, as demonstrated in the plethora of documented aberrations and sightings of her around the world to absolutely every culture. In the Akashic records we call on Mary to release past life patterns and habits. She brings forgiveness and opens up opportunities to begin again. One of the most profound things we have seen her do is pour holy oil on a cluster of energy that represents something we believe in that is no longer helpful or truthful. This "holy oil" seems to melt away the reasons we keep faithful to this belief and allows us to entertain a new idea. The freedom experienced from this compassionate act is tremendous and life-changing. If you find yourself trying to break free from a habitual thought or behavior it may be that it's held in place by something you believe in. It may be that this belief is unconscious. Call upon Mary to help you recognize what you are doing and pour her oil on it to set you free.

St. Germain

The Count of St. Germain (full name Comte de Saint Germain, 1712?–84), lived in Europe among royalty and was highly educated, extremely intelligent, wealthy, and quite eccentric even by French standards. We work with St. Germain because of his mastery with using transmutational energy. This energy, known as the violet flame, clears karma, spiritual toxins, and negative energy—and it is the best bar none. He can clear your entire Akashic record room of toxic energy in seconds. Molly Maid has nothing on St. Germain.

We were first introduced to St. Germain and the violet flame through the writing and teachings of Elizabeth Clare Prophet (1939–2009). Later, when we started working in the Akashic records, St.

Germain would come in and do some magnificent housekeeping (which at times was with a violet flamethrower, thank you very much). If you'd like to get to know this dynamic ascended master, invite him to tea in your Akashic records. He has a tremendous amount of knowledge to share.

Archangels

Reader Note: Our knowledge about angels comes from various sources, including Storm Cestavani, Rabbi Moshe Rosenberg, Whitney Hopler on About.com, *Archangels & Ascended Masters* by Doreen Virtue, PhD (Hay House, 2003), and *Secret Doors of the Qabala* by Ted Andrews (Dragon Hawk Publishing, 2007).

We have been working with the archangels since the beginning of our adventures in the Akasha, and we wouldn't have it any other way. These magnificent beings are pretty easy to work with, but it always helps to know their background and their area of expertise. We were taught from the get-go that these beings were designed to be filters of the Divine Light so we can experience it without total brain meltdown. They illuminate one subject at a time to help us wade through it. The archangels are also associated with the spheres on the Tree of Life. We have come to understand that the Kabbalah is another way to look at the Akashic records, but that is a whole other exciting way to learn and heal, and we will cover that in a future book!

We kept the archangel information simple so you can develop your own relationship with them and deepen your understanding on how they work within your Akashic records.

Metatron

Metatron, the "seed of God energy," is all about bringing order to chaos. He does this by planting a seed of a thought that gives you direction and purpose. When you need a do-over of great importance, Metatron is the guy to talk to. Call upon this archangel when you need help seeing through the distortions that can keep you from finding your core issues. Healing family legacies is one of Metatron's specialties.

Metatron is seen as a young boy who is most often crowned in light. You may also recognize that he is with you when you see a geometric shape with five points, petals, or sides in your records. Metatron is the leader of the archangels, so if you are unsure as to which angel to call upon, or what to do next, he will send in the perfect divine ally for you.

🖋 Life Lessons from Aunt Patty

In my husband's young life he was an alcoholic (which is also a family legacy). About a year into sobriety, he was teetering on a pretty nasty relapse. In desperation he prayed his heart out for divine intervention and surrendered like he'd never surrendered before. He called to Metatron to be his witness and release. It is my sincere belief that he was ready for his big do-over, and it was granted. If you find you have a major overhaul like this you'd like to do, call upon the big guy.

Ratziel

Ratziel, the "secret of God," gave the Book of Wisdom to Adam and Eve—not as a curse, but as a way for them to find their way back to the Divine once they started their journey out of the Garden of Eden. If you have come to the records because you feel totally lost in your life, call to Ratziel. He will bring the whole truth of a situation to help you gather knowledge and see the big picture of the issue. Bring to this archangel the damaged relationships with your father and father issues, especially where abuse happened.

Ratziel's symbol is the Book of Wisdom, and you will always find him with it in your Akashic records. You will also know him when you see an eternity symbol or images of standing stones.

Tzaphkiel

Tzaphkiel, the "knowledge of God," filters the light for us by showing us how God loves people. She shows us how to resolve conflicts, have compassion for each other, and understand our connections to each other. As the Divine Mother sphere on the Tree of Life, Tzaphkiel can assist in healing all mother issues and damaged relationships. Tzaphkiel's compassionate nature and dominion over karmic relationships help with the collection, return, and healing of disenfranchised (lost, wounded, or broken) soul parts.

Tzaphkiel's symbols represent the different gifts she can bring to you. As the healer of relationships, her symbol is the chalice or hand; as the sleuth and wise one, her symbol is the helmet; and as the watcher of the Divine, her symbol is the watchtower, where she brings an understanding to humanity. If you find yourself looking at your world from a cliff or high place, know that Tzaphkiel is guiding you.

✒ Jacki Jumps into the Kabbalah Deep End

I had a giant, life-changing aha moment that connected the Kabbalah, archangels, and the Akashic records. I saw how the top three spheres of the Tree of Life represent our own personal Akashic records, how the middle spheres (4–9) represent the process of manifesting this divine information, and how the last sphere (10) represents the physical world we live in. I began to understand how the Divine connects with us through the Kabbalah.

Metatron, Ratziel, and Tzaphkiel make up the top three spheres:

* Metatron is the storehouse of the records.

* Ratziel notes our actions, motivations, and intentions in the records.

Tzadkiel

Tzadkiel, the "righteousness of God," will expose the unjust, including you, if you are not repentant of your contribution to a conflict. He will help you find forgiveness of self and others in an unjust situation. Tzadkiel will also shore you up when you are caving to your impulses to be mean and nasty. (Hey, we all have our bad days.) He does this by healing our painful experiences and giving us some breathing room so we can stop acting out like caged animals. This is important, because without this gift it'll be all the harder to stop using negative thoughts and beliefs defensively. If we continue down that path, we will ultimately kick our own butts.

You will recognize Tzadkiel in your Akashic records when you see a white-haired old man. He will look a little like Oden, Zeus, or that typical image of God.

Khamael

Khamael, "he who seeks God," understands the workings of relationships and knows how to bring balance to any interactions between people. Khamael most often appears as a warrior in armor carrying a sword. Any warrior outfit will do for Khamael, be it Roman, Norse, medieval, or Robocop.

The way of the hero or warrior is always seeking the balance of love. Warriors are in place to resolve conflicts, and conflicts are so much easier to resolve when you have strength behind you. This is what Khamael is seen as, the angel of peaceful relationships and inner peace, so we may experience the positive and balanced side of relationships. Khamael will bring you skills, resources, and tools that you need to accomplish a difficult goal. He will support you on your journey and fight the battles that you are not equipped to handle.

Raphael

Raphael, "God heals," helps us cast out our own demons and maladies. Raphael can drive out the darkness that is causing dis-ease. His healing work starts with compassion for your struggle, making his healing gentle. This is not to say that Raphael hasn't performed miracles—he is known for this, he just does it without judgment, and that makes a difference. Raphael performs all types of healing: physical, mental, spiritual, and emotional. You've got demons of addiction and cravings to deal with? Call upon Raphael and watch those sissies run for the hills. His special blend of energy helps you rise above your limitations and struggles. Whatever weighs you down and prevents you from achieving your goals can be dealt with by Raphael.

Raphael is often seen with a staff, fish, and wings, which are ironically similar to the caduceus symbol found in healing centers. You will also see him working in cooperation with other archangels as he helps heal your issues.

Haniel

Call on Haniel, the "joy of God," to help you bring balance to your addictions or unbalanced behavior. She'll show you the wisdom of increasing your personal passion meter with endurance, fortitude, and patience. Haniel will be there to assist when you are ready to be victorious over your own self-sabotaging ways and bring joy and laughter into your life (also known as grace). Haniel is also a healer and the keeper of lost knowledge. She is always there to assist you in recovering the lost secrets of natural healing remedies and blending them with modern-day medical advances.

When you see an angel and you can't help but be calm, smile, and find the blessing in the situation, you are in the presence of Haniel. Just saying her name can bring a smile to your face. Haniel is represented by beauty in all forms and is most often seen as a beautiful woman or a very virile man. She carries a rose and a lantern to help uncover the joy and beauty in everything.

Michael

Michael, "he who is most like God?" and the rock star of the archangels, is your protector. His title of "he who is most like God?" ends in a question mark to remind us that we are all reflections of the Divine. Surrender your challenges to him. It's OK, uncurl your fingers and let go. When you are dealing with an entity or energy that is stronger than you, call to Michael to take authority over it. Michael trumps everything and will bring in the right helper if he is not the one for the job.

Michael is the most referenced archangel in the Bible. Although Metatron is the manager of all the archangels, Michael is said to be the first archangel and the defender of humanity. Michael helps rid us and the world of the toxins that are created by fear so we can recognize that divine reflection in ourselves and others.

Michael always comes to your aid when you call. You know it's Michael because he carries a shield, a flaming blue sword, and a chalice.

Gabriel

Gabriel, "God is my strength," is the bringer of revelations. She gives us a deeper understanding of how the Divine works in our world and through our lives. So expect an influx of smarty-pants energy to blow away confusion and bring clarity to any mental challenge you may have. Gabriel helps us to find our voice and learn how to communicate our ideas and message to the world in our own unique way. If you are at a loss for the right combination of words to convey your ideas perfectly, call to Gabriel to bring them to you. In fact, Gabriel has been writing this book right alongside us.

Gabriel is the sanctifier of earth, and she will destroy the lies and fears you have been using to color your world. She'll shake you up, wake you up, and keep you humble so you can grow, move, and elevate your spirit. You will recognize Gabriel when you hear her trumpet blow! Like Tzaphkiel, she carries many symbols representing the ways she can help: lanterns shine the truth; a mirror shows you what you are reflecting to the world; a shield and spear defend your voice; a lily brings peace; and a scepter lets you be the master of your world.

Sandalphon

Sandalphon, "co-brother," offers the miracle of forgiveness and transformation of the negative energy we create so we don't have to suffer the pain of living in our negativity. To be on the receiving end of this miracle we have to be truly repentant and show that we are trying to change our ways. Invite Sandalphon into your Akashic records anytime you need a swift, complete, and tangible change in your reality, such as with money issues, a career change, or physical problems. Show Sandalphon that you are willing to change your self-centered ways and he will help you with all his might.

Sandalphon's name "co-brother" represents that all of our life is co-created with the Divine. You will recognize him right away when you see his flaming chariot take your petitions up through the Tree of Life to the Divine. Sandalphon is the tallest of all the archangels, and he loves to travel with musical instruments, as they are the representation of what our actions create in our waking life.

Uriel

Uriel, whose name means "God is light," is the angel of wisdom. He shines the light of truth into the darkness of confusion. He is the curse-breaker and the truth serum. Call to Uriel in times of crisis and he will show you not only the truth of the situation but also possible resolutions to conflicts.

You will see Uriel with a scroll or a book and an open hand with a flame showing that he has the truth you need to get past the curse or karmic ties that are keeping you in the dark.

Lightworkers

Lightworkers is a title given to spirit guides within the New Age community. These guides are not affiliated with a deity, arch-angel, angel, or ascended master, but that doesn't mean they can't be any of those things. A lightworker is simply a great catch-all name for when we need a healer or energy technician but we don't know who to ask for specifically. Using the title lightworker puts out the intention that you need expertise in energy work or in a realm you are unfamiliar with, like other worlds. Think of it as a title or attainment, such as Buddha or ascended master.

Triage Repair Team

Think of this group of lightworkers as the MASH unit or emergency room nurses and doctors. We also call them the hazmat team and the detox team. After a healing (or during a healing, for that matter) you may need assistance in removing the toxic energy backlog from emotional hurts and mental crashes. These are the guys to call.

Aeons

Working with the aeons is fun, and they are very enthusiastic and efficient. They can be a big help when it comes to handling space problems, like containing a psychic opening in the aura. They can teach you about the nature of these openings, what they feel like, and how to recognize them when they pop open. For the most part, the aeons will close psychic openings for us—our job is to simply point them out and ask for help.

If you have second sight and you see some weird tunnel in your Akashic record room, you are looking into a portal. The guides may have put it there. Once you figure out what's going on, call the aeons to close the portal at both ends and repair the aura. They may need to help you clean up the energetic mess, too.

Only You Can Prevent Psychic Openings

Psychic openings (also called portals, doorways, or rips in the space-time continuum for you Trekkies) allow energy to flow from one dimension to another. Your aura, your friend's aura, Earth, the Akasha, this universe, and other universes are all dimensions. When this wall between the dimensions is compromised, it's like leaving the tap on in the tub; eventually the water will overflow and ruin the rug.

For example, say there's an opening between your aura and your friend's. Your energy flows into your friend's aura, and your friend's mind is all of a sudden filled with your thoughts, feeling, memories, and toxicity. They will feel like you are up in their business, and perhaps they have a migraine (where the portal is located often feels like an achy muscle).

When Things Get Weird, Call in the Aeons

We first met these lightworkers when we were in our sci-fi phase of Akashic exploration. For some reason the ongoing theme was lives lived on other planets or in spaceships and encounters of the otherworldly kind. Most of the issues we wrestled with were about being victimized, disempowered, terrorized, and enslaved. One of the first ways the aeons helped us was to relieve us of old devices that were implanted long, long ago by people we no longer knew. The energy of these long-gone beings still caused us great pain, confusion, and a good case of the stoopids in this life. Some of our sessions boiled down to pointing out an unidentifiable energy mass in the aura and asking the aeons to take it out. With gentleness and great fascination they went to work and the aura or chakra was cleared in no time. This sci-fi experience may not be what you find in your Akashic records, but you can still call upon the aeons if you come across something strange and you don't know what to do with it.

Sacred Elders

The sacred elders are magnificent beings who work on the spiritual layer of our aura. They help our bodies heal by making changes in our spiritual body that will be felt in the physical body in good time. (Now there's a trickle-down economy you can count on!) We often ask them to heal our physical body after we've released our hurt and learned our lesson. We generally invite the sacred elders to work on us once all the counseling and sorting out of the details is done, and we have let go of the past and are ready to embrace new perspectives and launch new spiritual habits and behaviors.

The sacred elders' work will help prevent a negative pattern that you are still in the process of letting go from manifesting again in your body. They will also let the body know the negative pattern is resolved and no longer interfering with the body's ability to heal. Then the miracle of self-healing kicks in.

Other Guides

We can't neglect the oddball guides that show up as cartoon characters, archetypes from the tarot, and characters from pop culture. These guides are so much fun, and they bring poignant lessons besides.

Some of the guides we've worked with come from religions from all over the world. Pagan, Roman, and Greek gods and goddesses teach us about strength, sacrifice, and becoming a hero. The archetypes from the tarot help us with challenges we're having in just growing up. Cartoon characters bring levity. And our favorite, the cast from *The Wizard of Oz*, embodies the lessons around building personal character and morality. No matter who shows up in your Akashic records, be assured you will not forget them easily.

All of the guides, whether you experience them as family, forms of energy, or your favorite superhero, are there on your behalf to enlighten you. You will never experience an agenda coming from any of these guides that is personal to them or self-serving. If you are being manipulated, guilted, or pushed around, you are dealing with a dark teacher. These teachers love the school of hard knocks and are quite the task masters. You don't have to face this kind of teacher by yourself and well you shouldn't. Please call upon a lightworker guide from our list to help you.

Chapter 9

It Really Is All about You—
The Girl's Got Soul

Every day, through every trauma and every emotional experience, we shed a few soul parts or trade them out for another. We do this to shield ourselves or to establish a connection with others and get access to their energy or allow them access to ours. After a while, the energy exchanges can become a jumbled mess, and we need some TLC to get back on track. This chapter takes you on a journey that will help you to reconnect with your lost soul parts, clear the soul pieces that don't belong to you, and heal and realign your soul. The meditations included here will leave you tuned up, energized, empowered, and stronger when you are done.

What Is a Soul?

In western African cosmology, each person is believed to be a new incarnation from the sea of souls. Each time someone is born, their new soul is made up of parts from that sea of souls. We are gifted with the wisdom of experiences those souls had in their past lives and incarnations. And when we die, we become a drop in that sea of souls and contribute to the whole again, spread out and indiscernible in this sea until we are born again with parts of a new soul.

Each soul begins its journey smooth and whole, but every experience of pain, cruelty, or diversion from its destiny takes a chunk out, and over time it becomes misshapen. It is said, by the Africans, to live your life keeping the sides as smooth as possible is to live a life of blessing to the tribe. The shaman's goal for his tribesmen was to bring cracked and chipped souls back their original quality by smoothing them out and putting the pieces back together. The shamans would do this with their healing work, but also by having their tribesmen do types of actions that would help others and start to fill their souls back in.

The tribe's members would wear soul stones with a hole in the middle on rawhide strips around their ankles as a reminder to keep their soul as pure as possible. This was also protection against others who would attack their soul. It was hoped that the stone would remind everyone that damage to another person also damages their own soul. This tradition means so much to the people of western Africa they still wear soul stones today.

This is just one of the many theories on how incarnation happens, and they all contribute to the main question: What is our purpose on earth, and what happens when we die? We won't debate creation theories; we will just do our best to begin to understand how to deal with what is in front of us.

Here's another cool idea. Let's say our life is part of a larger oversoul, where all the memories of the lifetimes lived before are kept. If we look at this oversoul as our own personal sea of souls, we can begin to understand the potential magnitude of experiences we can draw from to learn about or heal something. Since not all of our soul incarnates each time (we are just that magnanimous), each incarnation contributes priceless details to our soul's journey. Having an oversoul that collects all the data from our individual lifetimes kinda sounds like our own Akashic records.

The mysteries of Spirit are what keep us striving and growing and evolving! It's exciting and life-changing when we start to glimpse a few of our own mysteries!

What Is a Soul Part?

We hinted at soul parts in the last chapter on guides and helpers in the Akashic realm, but we're going to elaborate here. Our soul craves experiences, and we often need protection from the more brutal ones. Soul fracturing is an automatic way we can have these kinds of experiences and still be able to carry on. We can break off a piece of ourselves and attach it to the emotional pain and leave it free to float in our aura like rings around Saturn. A soul part is a piece of that free-floating spirit. It goes "out of body" and stays there, encompassing the event and emotional reactions to it for us and hangs out in our unconscious. This helps our consciousness or waking awareness move on in our life.

We fracture our soul when we don't have the skills, the awareness, the self-love, or the forgiveness needed to handle a particular situation in the moment. Other times we plan to designate, or sacrifice, a part of our soul to experience a trying event, record it, and take it back to the Akasha to be documented and learned from.

Later, after we've grown and gotten wiser, we can go back to heal the residual pain, judgments, and beliefs. When we go back to review and heal the trauma of an experience, we can view it from a perspective that allows for forgiveness, compassion for ourselves and others, and clarity on why we agreed to an experience and what was to be learned and gained by doing it.

✒ A Soul-Fracturing Tale from the Akashic Records

A woman marries a man who, she learns too late, isn't really in love with her but is using her to gain something for himself. She is devastated, but she chooses to stay with him for reasons that have nothing to do with love and everything to do with using him right back. Over time, with every hurtful interaction between the woman and her husband, she fractures a piece of herself off to carry that pain so she can maintain her decision to stay with him. She is also fracturing off a piece of her self-esteem, personal power, and light.

This is why when we stay in abusive or manipulative relationships we feel like the life is being drained out of us. It's not exactly drained off, but held captive within these soul parts and pieces and stored in the unconscious, unavailable until they are triggered by something. When a soul part is triggered, we experience whatever emotions and beliefs are stored there. This is when we can experience the "seeing red" rage and why we can have such over-the-top reactions to new events that resonate with the original wound. Behind those feelings are our beliefs and the power held captive by them.

Give and Take: Why We're So Free with Our Stuff

I give a little and you take a lot. That's how it feels, at least. When we feel threatened, jealous, out of control, or lonely, there is a hair-trigger coping mechanism we can pull to keep the peace in our little world, and that is called soul part swapping. Below are the four basic ways and reasons we end up with someone else's soul parts and they end up with ours.

Look, a Monkey: The Diversion Soul Swap

Being overly helpful out of fear, possessiveness, rigidness, and codependence diverts our parts and pieces to someone else instead of storing our soul parts in our unconscious or our Akasha. Most of the time we do this because we are attempting to find comfort, be cared for, hide—and, on the more dramatic side—be possessed, controlled, and manipulated. Other times we are forcing a connection with another person to continue unfinished business from a past life, or we're acting out on an obsession. This happens when we don't believe in ourselves and wish to abdicate our life and destiny to another.

The Prenuptial Soul Swap

Sometimes we give away a piece of ourselves because we think we will be better liked or loved, or our act of sacrifice will calm the beast we are dealing with in an abusive relationship. This is a very typical interaction in family scenarios. An insecure wife will do this kind of underground maneuvering to keep her husband happy and at home. Unfortunately, we see it between parent and child, too.

The Soul-Sucking Vampire Soul Swap

Just as we can give pieces of our soul away to others, sometimes we can grab parts of other people's souls, and it's usually for the same reasons: we want control and influence, and we want their energy. To intentionally take advantage of someone's fears and weaknesses creates karmic debt that has to be balanced and paid back eventually. Besides, it's not nice.

The Martyr Soul Swap

The converse can happen too. We can take on or inherit someone else's soul part in an attempt to carry their burdens, comfort them, and even try to heal them. Yes, there is an agreement here between the two souls to interact with each other in this way, but we are all accountable and responsible for our actions.

No matter how your soul parts have been lost, gained, mixed, and matched over the years, you can straighten things out with the help of the Akashic records.

Is That a Soul Part in Your Pocket, or Are You Just Happy to See Me?

Before you can heal a soul part, you need to be able to identify one. Soul parts come in many stages of completion. A soul part could look like a floating, disembodied head—the full monty— or it could be as scattered and vague as fairy dust, or burnt shoe leather. A good rule of thumb is, the more "stuff" that is present, the more energy is locked up in what you see. The wispy, sparkling parts are barely there and can be cleared out without any drama. Those are fragments of a story. Think of them as shrapnel from an emotional bomb that went off long ago. When you find a soul part taking up space in your Akashic records, invite the goddess Kwan Yin to pop over and assist you. Stay tuned. More on how to deal with broken and lost soul parts to come.

Soul parts can be any age and come from any past life you've traversed. The soul parts that look like a younger version of you are called wounded inner children, adolescents, or adults, depending on their age. Notice how they are dressed, how tidy or dirty they are, and their body language; these things will show you the beginning of their story.

Everything you experience about a soul part is a message for you, so pay attention and don't take anything for granted. We also have seen inner children that are called "the magical child." The magical child, is the part of you that has retained its innocence and deep wisdom from your higher self. Whenever you see your magical child there is a beautiful teaching coming your way. This child is delightful, cute, and glows with the love and grace of the Divine. You just want to pick them up and squeeze them.

Soul parts from your past lives look the part. They wear period clothing and focus entirely on where they are from and who they are. Getting their story is fascinating.

We said that sometimes you can have soul parts that aren't your own. The soul parts that belong to people in your life like your parents, kids, friends, coworkers, bosses, etc., will be hanging around in various stages of lucidity. Sometimes you will be able to see the face of the soul part's owner; others you will just know whose it is. Occasionally, your guide will need to identify a soul part's owner for you.

You will perceive the soul parts in your record room in different ways, so don't discount the "knowing" or that you can smell them. It's not uncommon to feel the soul parts' emotions. In fact, at first, you may mistake them for your emotions. A stuck soul part can also be felt in your body as a phantom pain or cool breeze inside of you.

✒ Soul Connections with Aunt Patty

Nine times out of ten, the wounded soul part healings I do with clients center around helping them disentangle from a tricky family relationship. During this particular session, it was no different.

My client came in looking for help getting traction in his life, and left minus one giant soul part of his dad's. As we looked at the different challenges he was having, I kept seeing this cranky, disapproving old man hanging out in his Akashic record room. *That's his dad, of course,* I thought to myself. But I had to figure out a way to help my client see that his dad was the block to his successful future.

My client did not make the connection between his dad and his failures in life. Once I was able to get his dad's soul part isolated and silenced, my client had the space to think for himself and see that his dad was not the advocate he thought he was.

Removing my client's dad's soul part helped him let go of trying to please a father who was so afraid junior would fail he started to expect it. That powerful expectation turned into fear, and poor, disillusioned Pops attached that fear and sent it over to my client in a soul part swap. This was hard for my client to come to terms with, but he understood where his father was coming from and forgave him. My client was able to get his career going after that, and he learned to be more protective of himself where his father was concerned.

Akashic Tales from Aunt Jacki

Jean came to me on a recommendation, and when we sat down to begin the session, there was no time for questions because her mother's soul parts were guarding the door to her Akashic record room. Thank goodness your door is connected to the room, because we needed to begin the healing session there in front of the door. It was clear I was going to help my client find her own identity.

I described the motherly energy that I saw, and Jean immediately started crying. At fifty-five years old, her mother was still trying to call the shots in Jean's life, and she was now trying to separate Jean from her husband. I took Jean back to the moment when her mother's soul parts began blocking Jean's Akashic records so we could look at this from the original intention and clear it from there.

What we discovered was an infant Jean close to death with meningitis, while her mother prayed and offered her life and soul for the life of her baby. Jean had only seen her mother as controlling and manipulating and never as a woman who cared so much; this gave her a new perspective on her mother's behavior. The original intention that caused a swapping of soul parts got distorted over the years into an exaggerated sense of responsibility on the part of Jean's mother. Mom was trying to live both of their lives at the same time.

We asked to change the moment when Jean's mom was about to plant her soul parts in her baby to having Archangel Raphael bless baby Jean with his healing energy. Then we asked that this shift of energy cascade forward in time to the day I was working with Jean. This released Jean and her mother from the contract that was created during this moment of panic. We also asked that Archangel Raphael make his presence known to Jean's mother in her time of stress to bring her comfort and peace.

After the healing, Jean called to say that it took time to change everyone's spiritual habits, but her mother was not trying to control her life anymore. She knew the clearing had worked when one day her mother said to her, "I have always known angels were watching out for you." That was the first time her mother had ever said that to her.

What a Freaking Mess, Call in the Goddesses

Thank the stars above we don't have to sort out soul parts on our own. Remember that we have many goddesses and guides who can help. Here is a quick list, but refer back to chapter 8 for further instructions on how to work with them.

Kwan Yin, the goddess of compassion, is the first one to call upon for all soul retrieval work. She guides soul parts back to the body they belong to or back home to the Divine if they are too wounded to heal (we call those soul parts crispy critters).

Lilith is our champion when we need help extricating our soul parts from dangerously aggressive relationships and contracts. As the advocate and rescuer of abused children and women, Lilith will not hold back when her talents are needed.

Brigid is your goddess to call upon if you need to clear soul part cling-ons that are causing confusion and distraction. She clears away what is ready to go without fanfare.

Kali is the perfect goddess for those wounded soul parts with karmic connections that just won't budge. Kali is not gentle in her extraction, but sometimes the Band-Aid needs to be ripped off.

Tzaphkiel is the archangel to call upon when the soul parts in question are based on karmic relationships, especially romantic relationships.

Haniel is the archangel to call upon when jealousy is the dominant emotion involved or when there is a fear of being empty and not needed when you let go of the soul parts that don't belong to you.

No matter who you call upon, Kwan Yin is your first go-to goddess. She will get assistance as needed.

Meditation: Clearing Other People's Soul Parts from Your Akashic Records

Carrying around others' soul parts makes you tired and clouds your thoughts and emotions. It makes good sense to let go of what doesn't belong to you. When you take on other people's broken soul parts, you also run the risk of taking on their karma. That's motivation enough right there.

To start, enter your Akashic record room using either the quick and dirty method or the formal method in chapter 5. Once you are in your Akashic record room, take a few deep, cleansing breaths and state your intention for visiting your Akashic records. For the purposes of this meditation, we're going to state: "I would like to release all the soul parts that don't belong to me."

As you look around your room, you may see evidence of the soul parts you've been carrying around with you. They may be standing around in a group, or you may see dust or bubbles with faces in them. Be open to the way your guides show you the soul parts that are hanging out with you.

Once you've taken an inventory of your soul parts, start organizing them. Ask your guides to separate your soul parts from the ones that don't belong to you. You may see soul parts from family members, friends, acquaintances, and strangers—even people from different times.

Invite Archangel Michael to cut the cords that are connecting you to the outsiders' soul parts.

Next, call in Kwan Yin and Lilith to collect all the foreign soul parts and return them to their own Akashic record rooms.

Thank your guides, Archangel Michael, and the goddesses for their help, and leave your Akashic records. Go back through the door in your heart chakra and return to your waking life.

You can stop here or do the next meditation.

We've been asked if it's OK to keep the broken or wounded soul parts of the people we love and are taking care of, like kids and aging parents. Sorry, but the answer is no. Take care of your loved ones in real time and do it consciously. The broken soul parts we inherit will hang out in our unconscious, and we are ill-equipped to be of any help there, because we are, after all, unconscious. This means we are not aware of the presence of a soul part that needs help. The best place for broken soul parts is with their human, their oversoul, or God.

Meditation: Retrieving and Healing Your Soul Parts

There will be some soul parts that are ready to be healed and return to you the power and talents they hold. Then you'll find others that are so done, they are unresponsive and quite crispy. You will be guided to let them go back to Spirit and then asked to be filled with replacement energy from your spirit. This meditation will help you update your soul part cache.

*

Close your eyes and take a deep cleansing breath, remembering your connection to Spirit and the earth. Bring your focus back to your heart chakra and find the door to your room. Open the door and enter your room.

Now it's time to heal your own soul parts that hold wounds from this lifetime. Ask your guides to separate your soul parts into two groups. The first group is all your soul parts that need to go back to Spirit because they are unable to heal and remerge with you, or they have fulfilled their contract and it's time for them to go. The second group is all your soul parts that need to heal and rejoin you and return power back to you.

Invite Kwan Yin to collect all the soul parts that are going home, and put them on the soul train to heaven. As you watch them go, release all the toxic energy that surrounded them. Let your imagination tell you how this is handled. Maybe the energy goes into the fire of a cauldron that has magically appeared here for you to use. Maybe it is released out of your aura and floats into the air. Maybe it falls to the floor and is swept up into the dustpan. Just let it all go.

Now invite your higher self to bring in the light or energy or soul substance that you need to replace what was just given back to your oversoul. Allow it to fill you wherever it is needed. Breathe it in. Allow the wisdom of your Akashic records do this for you.

Shift your attention to the group of soul parts that are waiting to be healed and rejoin you. Ask your guides to select one perfect soul part for this meditation right here and right now.

Kwan Yin is here again with three gifts for you: a color, a quality (like courage), and a thing. Let the color fill the soul part's aura, empowering and revitalizing it. Let the quality fill its heart, healing it of its pain. And put the thing in its hands, preparing it to rejoin your incarnated soul. Watch as your soul part changes, heals, and comes alive with a desire to be free of its wound.

Now ask for a message from this newly healed soul part. Once you have the message, ask your soul part if it's ready to rejoin you and see this life out together.

Allow this soul part to move toward you and enter your aura and then your heart. Merge together smoothly and gracefully and fully. Kwan Yin will assist you where you need it. Just allow it to happen as you are surrounded by the wisdom of your Akashic records and guides.

Now that you know how to do this you can continue your work with the rest of your soul parts.

Take a deep cleansing breath, thank Kwan Yin and your guides, and shift your awareness to the doorway between your records and your waking life.

Move toward the door, walk through it, and become aware of your body; feel it, move it, wiggle your toes, and take a deep breath.

Come more fully aware of the room. Open your eyes. Welcome back.

✒ Tools on the Fly: The Cauldron

The cauldron came about when a client needed her Akashic records to be erased. We had found the fear and cleared it, but there were many decisions the client had made based on her fears. They were no longer valid, but they were still recorded and hanging out. We asked that those parts of her records be cleared forever, and they were, but that wasn't enough for her. She wanted a ritual burning of the records and to scatter the ashes. A cauldron appeared with the eternal flame within it. She fed her records into the flames, and they burnt to a place where they couldn't be resurrected. She felt so empowered by this and complete in her healing. We have used the cauldron several times in our own sessions and sessions with clients. It is a cathartic ritual that we need every now and again.

Finding Our Shadow Self

We are a delightfully mixed-up collage of light and dark, of enlightenment and searching. And to quote Djuna Barnes, author of *Nightwood,* "A man is whole only when he takes into account his shadow as well as himself." It's what makes us interesting.

Our shadow self is where the aspects of our personality we are unconscious of hang out. Letting the unconscious mind do the driving is never a good idea—it's too detached from real life. We want to bring balance to the light and the dark within us, but does that mean that our shadow self is fraught with everything we don't like about our self? The potential is very high, but among our more sinister qualities there are sure to be a lot of heroic ones as well. You have some good traits in your shadow self you don't even know about—yet.

For all you skeptics out there, we acknowledge that there are many seekers who question the validity of the dark side or the shadow self. The challenging spiritual inquiry becomes: "Where is God in the darkness?" There is too much pain and fear here for us to believe that this darkness is useful and will help us do anything but suffer. Without complete understanding of what the shadow side is about, we can and will torment ourselves with our judgments about it.

As with many things we don't understand, we deal with it by either denying its existence or trying to kill it. Truth be told, what we resist persists, and if we want to tame our shadow self, we will need to make friends with it and manage it. Those of us who fight the hardest to squelch the shadow end up demonizing it. What that means is that we have given the shadow the power to influence our reality. We have broken with what's real and have begun living our nightmare. Our way back from this insanity is to take back the desire to abdicate to our shadow self and integrate its qualities into our awareness.

Message from Mother Mary

Your shadow self is also your God self. It is there so you can express your free will and make personal choices. To judge that the shadow is not God is to reject a beautiful and powerful part of yourself. You need this part of you that thinks it is not one with God so that you can question God. It is healthy to do this. It is what inspires creativity, which means to give of yourself. Rather than judge, use your shadow self to evolve and develop your individuality.

This is also where your ego lives. This doesn't mean your ego *is* your shadow self; but in order for you to activate your personal preferences you need to know who you are. You need your shadow self to challenge what is already in place, no matter who put it there—yes, even God. Without challenging the status quo you can become stagnated and stop your evolution.

Many of us have used our shadow self as a dumping ground for everything we dislike about ourselves. This makes it harder and harder to embrace and love our shadow. Eventually, our emotional rejection of this part of ourselves throws us so out of balance that we have wild aversions to any expression of individuality. We have a hard time feeling safe every time we are faced with something that is different from us or our beliefs. The larger and darker our shadows gets, the more our light dims, and life is seen as dangerous. We even begin to fear our own power. This is how jealousy, competition, and prejudice take root.

This gentle yet empowering description of our shadow self helps us both see the beauty and strength to be had in our challenges, and parts of us that we don't think are valuable. Mary takes it one giant step further and points out again that there is no place that is not loveable, forgivable, valuable, and useful.

So what do we do to take that courageous step of embracing our shadow self and bring ourselves back into balance? We're very glad you asked. Deal with an overwhelming shadow self like you would any attention-starved and bored child: pay attention to it and give it something to do.

✒ A Tip from Aunt Patty

Emptying out our shadow self cache won't happen with one trip to the records. It will take a significant amount of soul searching and willingness to look at some things we have skillfully hidden from ourselves. Please don't be discouraged if you can't get very far with this. Often, this is an area where we need another set of eyes to look at us objectively and call us on our BS—in a loving and supportive way, of course.

Akashic Healing of Your Shadow Self

Begin your shadow self management project as if organizing for a yard sale. The first thing you'll be doing is inventory and evaluation, so go into your records and ask to be shown what you've thrown in the back of the closet that is contributing to your fears and anger about your life. Then start three piles: keep, sell, and recycle. (We always recycle in the Akashic realm.)

Keep

The items in the keep pile are the things, events, or memories that represent your ability to be powerful in your life. This is stuff like: the time you stood up for yourself, spoke your mind, valued your uniqueness, showed discernment, a glowing report card or job review, an award of any kind, a gift from a best friend or someone who believed in you, or a tough lesson that made you a better person, to name a few.

Recycle

The pile that gets recycled contains other people's stuff you've collected or inherited that is now pretty useless as is. Start with ideas and beliefs that are not in alignment with who you are. Then move on to that stack of shame because you didn't meet someone's expectations and dump it into the recycle bin. Now you're rolling. Out with other people's broken soul parts, addictions, habits, beliefs, opinions or willfulness, the "you should" and "that's the way we do it around here, so get with the program" pieces of advice that have been forced on you or you have accepted for any reason—including things you've inherited in your DNA or cultural/familial/social programming. Oh and that bad habit of twirling your hair when you're nervous you picked up from your mother?—toss it into the recycle bin. Any beliefs that came from your parents or grandparents (check out family legacies in chapter 10) go in the recycle bin too. If something no longer fits, if it makes you feel unappreciated or undervalued, or if it contributes to your dissatisfaction in yourself in any way, into the recycle bin it goes.

Sell

The pile that goes to the yard sale is the miscellaneous stuff that has value but you don't have room for in your life any longer, such as that bucket list that doesn't resonate with who you have become. You don't have to follow through on the promise made to go bungee jumping in the Grand Canyon just because it sounded like a rad time when you were sixteen. The idea here is to let what turns you on change and still be OK with yourself. You're not a failure because you've changed your mind or grown out of being a thrill seeker. Your goal here is to loosen up some energy by letting go of (recycling) some of the ideas that may have seemed good at the time but you will not be following through on. Consider selling a few vows, too. Someone will find them useful. Remember, one person's trash is another person's treasure. Oh—and no selling off disenfranchised soul parts. It's illegal.

A few trips back to this project will give you the space to think about your choices and process your reactions. Go ahead and ask a trusted friend who has a reputation of being honest with you about what you found and what pile you put it in. Sometimes we put stuff in the keep pile and it really belongs in the recycle bin. We feel loyal to our stuff, and if it was a gift, we may worry we are disrespecting someone if we say no thank you. It's OK if you don't want to keep Grandpa Joe's addiction to cigarettes. I'm sure he'll understand that it's nothing personal when you recycle that gift.

When you have made your final decisions and everything is in its proper pile, go back into your records and call upon your guides to help you place all the energy where it belongs.

At this point in your record room, notice how the keeper pile has now been placed in your consciousness as gifts and tools to help you in your waking life. The yard sale stuff has been moved to the great Akashic flea market in the sky. And the recycling bin will soon be taken away to the big recycling plant to be repurposed into new, positive things for other people to use. Remember, your stuff is only energy—it can change hands and morph in appearance, but it cannot be created or destroyed.

You've done some phenomenal and deeply healing work and have earned a huge pat on the back. Take a deep cleansing breath and look around your room. Was anything left behind, or is it tidy? If you find that a few items still lay there, you will need to find out what is keeping them here. Leave it for another day and go out and celebrate your good work.

Past Selves, Past Lives: When You Wish upon a Star, Makes No Difference Who You Are

If you're the type who says the past is the past and you choose to ignore it and bury it, you are missing out on a very powerful tool in your healing. Our past experiences hold a treasure trove of gifts that will not only explain who we have become, they are the keys to exorcising our dysfunctions, fears, and phobias.

When we heal our past, we reclaim all the self-esteem and power we've locked up in trauma, guilt, and misunderstandings. Our past experiences also shed a welcome light on why we do the crazy things we do in this lifetime. In *Many Lives, Many Masters* by Brian L. Weiss, MD, we learn how phobias could be linked directly to a traumatic event in a past life. When Dr. Weiss regressed his patients to that past life and they remembered the event, they awoke free of the phobia because it was no longer an unknown. They knew exactly what they were afraid of and they knew what happened to them.

In your Akashic records you will find past selves and past lives. Your past self is an earlier time within your current life. This past self dealt with life differently than how you currently react to your environment. For example, waiting for dessert as a five-year-old is very different from waiting for dessert at your current age; in your twenties your level of personal responsibility is different than it is once you are in your forties. These past selves may no longer be in your resident memory, but they hold many clues to why you react to some stimuli in your life.

Your past lives are a horse of a different color (and a buggy, too). Past lives are literally lives you lead in a different time, with a different name, different circumstances, and probably even a different gender.

Whether you are looking at a past self or a past life, your guides will let you know that it's time to reflect on past events by projecting a hologram of a character from a different time in your room. The first thing that gives it away is the clothing. Next you may be shown a book with a date on it, or invited to watch a historical documentary on the big screen. This character and movie are all answers to a question you brought to the Akasha.

To learn from a past self, ask your guides to run the movie of that lifetime to help you identify the repeating belief, mindset, or unresolved experience that is carrying over into your current life. If the movie stalls, ask to skip to the next important scene. You may only get pieces of the movie like snippets of memories, but after awhile you will be able to put all the scenes together to understand the message they came to give you. With this information you have the opportunity to see the root cause of your issue and begin to heal it.

Maybe a movie isn't necessary. Try talking to this hologram and see if it can give you the message it came to give. It may be cryptic or piecemeal, but keep with it until you understand how this character from your past is impacting your current life.

Learning from a past self is similar to learning from a past life—only this time you are familiar with all the players, and your goal is to gain a new perspective on the past. You will be able to change the past by healing from that past self forward. When you clear a soul part, block, fear, contract, etc., from the moment of its creation, you are able to carry that healing forward and change the outcomes you are experiencing today. For example, clearing a fear of dogs that started in childhood will change your attitude about dogs today. Working in the Akashic records to help heal your past negative experiences will shift your perspective, and you'll be able to react differently the next time you encounter a similar experience.

The more you work with the Akasha, the more you will see that answers come in many forms, and questions are rarely directly answered. You are a riddle to be solved, and that means following hints and clues. Don't fret; you will always have help along the way.

Past Life Storytime with Aunt Patty

I went to the Akashic records to get help with understanding my husband and our marriage. I was shown several lifetimes where my husband and I let our personal problems and prejudices interfere with our ability to connect and really get to know each other and let love grow between us.

Over and over again I was shown how I pushed him away even though he was committed to me and really loved me. I also saw how I was still harboring resentment over past mistakes and hurts. I came away with the understanding that my husband, for better or worse, has always loved me and his loyalty is something I can trust and count on.

Since nobody is perfect and he's got his own stuff to work out, I realized I was faced with a choice. I could decide to forgive him (and forgive myself) and let him be human, or I could use past transgressions as an excuse to block the love he has for me and perpetuate my wounds while saddling him with being responsible for my happiness. When I looked at it that way, I could see where I was the saboteur this go around.

OK, what do you do with that past self or past life experience? You've been given the gift of remembrance; now uplift that past self so it becomes an ally to you.

Finding Compassion and Healing Your Past Self

In your records, your journey has brought to you a past self or past life. Ask your guides to play that story out on the big screen. Ask about who you were, what happened back then, and how it's still affecting you today. Your new understanding will open up a new choice for you: Do you walk away and shut the door on the past, or do you offer yourself a healing?

Your guides will help you understand what your next step is. If the movie about your past life turns off and the screen goes dark, then you are ready to release that past life by understanding, forgiving yourself, and releasing the emotions from that lifetime. Your guides will close and seal the door to that past life for you, only opening it again if you need to address a new layer of healing from that lifetime.

If the movie about your past life keeps playing, then you have a bit more work to do. Trauma from that past life is bleeding over into this one, and your guides want you to bring empowerment to the past self that was victimized. You will fill it with love, compassion, and a gift that will help it overcome the trauma and resulting fears and beliefs that had been screwing up your life today.

Tools on the Fly: The Gift

When we come across a scary and difficult issue that stops our clients in their tracks, there is always a gift or resource that gives the ability to get through the issue. There was a client whose inner child was dealing with a scary cousin who would intimidate her and thought it was funny. This issue within her records was manifesting in her waking life as an inability to handle any confrontations. We asked for a gift for her inner child. She got a red ball, but it was no ordinary red ball, it was a ball that she could chase her cousin away with. We were confused by the red ball until she opened her eyes in her living room and there was a picture of a dragon holding a red ball. She became the dragon. Don't judge the gift, just use it.

Here is the miraculous, exciting part: In helping yourself in a past life, you will be creating an alternate outcome in that lifetime for your past self that will bring the needed love, compassion, skill, or strength to you in this lifetime. Ask your guide to bring one, two, or three gifts for you to give to your past self. They are gifts that will provide healing for your past self as well as an opportunity for something different to happen. The other key players in the issue that is being healed may be impacted as well.

What this does is soften its influence on your current life and bring forward more optimism and creativity to you. We often see a color, a quality (like integrity), and a thing (something that represents the healing power) presented by the guide. Once you have received the gifts, present them to your past self. Watch what they do with the gifts and how they change because of them. These really are gifts you are giving yourself, and since you are giving them to the you that experienced the original wound, the healing begins there.

Next watch how the empowering gifts change the scene or the way the people act or change. These are all indications of how the energy is shifting, and it will have an impact on every lifetime that you have worked on this lesson. How this past self heals and feels about themselves is how you and your current situation will heal.

This bit of healing is done, and now you can thank your past self and your guides for the fine work. Allow that past life to recede into the background; close the door, and never open it unless more constructive work is to be done.

Prepare to leave your records or work with your guides on another topic that interests you.

✒Another Epic Tale from Aunt Patty

During a healing I found myself a captive of an enemy tribe. I had been tied to a tree and beaten. In that life I was young, female, and helpless, and completely overpowered by these men. I didn't see any way out and waited to die. This level of disempowerment affected me so deeply I carried a version of it through many lifetimes, and it was contributing to my shyness and discomfort in public speaking in this life.

I was guided to go to the tree with three gifts: the color pink for love, a eagle feather to help her speak, and courage to help her stand up for herself. As I gave the three gifts to this young woman, she was clearly affected by them. She got up, her wounds healed spontaneously, and she was filled with a sense of eternalness that no one could take away from her, no matter what happened to her body. She began to glow with her divinity and her dignity.

Beyond her the men began to change, too. Even though they didn't see her transformation, they began to question their own behavior and collectively decided that to imprison and kill this girl was wrong.

This is the power of bringing positive energy (light) into a dark and negative place. My past was changed and sent waves of change out and through to today. I can say that I am much more comfortable with public speaking and my shyness is not as much of a liability as it used to be.

Changing Your Past

The past is created by our perceptions of it. We all have a different story of what happened when the dog knocked over the Ming vase. Your mother remembers that you got the dog riled up. Your father remembers you opening the door for the dog when he said not to. You remember that the last time you let the dog scratch at the back door instead of letting him in you got in trouble. You remember that your parents were arguing about something, so you ignored them and let the dog in.

The reason why you remember this so vividly is that you were mortified that no matter what you did you were yelled at. Your mother had passed on and your father barely remembers even owning that vase. Go into your past and change it; go outside with the dog to play or go into the bathroom first. Maybe tell your parents to stop yelling at you. You can even send your current or future self to that moment and shield your past self from the trauma.

As we just demonstrated in the last meditation, you can change the past to effect change in your life today. Since there is no time or space in the Akashic dimension, healings, changes, and energy shifts will be available in real time. All it takes is making a new choice, changing your perspective, believing in yourself, deciding to forgive, understanding your sacrifice, and allowing divine intervention to work on your behalf.

✒ Akashic Tales from Aunt Jacki

I had a client who suffered from a perpetual cough. Just a little *cough cough* every few minutes that wouldn't go away. All the tests her doctors ran came back normal; she is a healthy girl (then and now). She came to me to see if there was something in her records.

We were immediately taken back to a past life where she was stabbed in the throat. In that life she was a warrior who was sparring with someone who in this life she was dating. Confused yet? As a warrior she was accidently killed and the soul that killed her was caught in a karmic loop of trying to make it up to her.

The soul part from that life hung on to the trauma because they thought the other warrior dealt the fatal blow on purpose. The other warrior was roaring with success, not realizing that they just killed their sparring partner. We were able to change the past by delaying her death a few minutes so the other warrior could react in horror at what they did and beg forgiveness before she died. She was able to forgive them, releasing both souls from this repeating drama.

Her cough was gone by the time the healing session was done. You can change your past and have it affect your present.

Using your past lives to help you heal today is a powerful tool, and when you heal the past, you are healing much more than today's incarnation. You will be sending healing energy into every life that was created in an effort to right or balance what happened in the root lifetime. It's a miracle, and it's magical to watch.

Maybe changing your past seems like a ruse. How can you change your past? You can't un-ring a bell!

The healing that comes from changing the past is in your acceptance of what happened, understanding who you really are while letting go of who you (or others) thought you were, and releasing damaging and limiting emotions, thoughts, and beliefs that were born out of that happening.

What you are changing is the vibration of the energy from that past life so that it no longer broadcasts into your life and colors the way you feel about yourself and the world. With this kind of healing you will shift from carrying around a burden to proudly sporting a badge of courage.

Chapter 10

The People We Meet on the Akashic Street

You would think that your Akashic room would be your sanctuary and quite devoid of other people unless you invited them for a little party or card game, but alas, they can pop in and linger until you find out what's up. No worries; when you see people, they are holographic projections, not the real McCoy, so don't feel like your security has been breached and folks have run amok in your room. You are still calling the shots here. But before you send them away in a huff, find out why your guides—or even you, for that matter—have called their likeness to your room. There is always a reason why, a message to be heard and a lesson to be learned, so take advantage of the vision and its timeliness. You can bet your booty that this visit is not random.

It is said that the five people you spend the most time with in your life influence you the most, so don't be surprised if they have a starring role in some of your Akashic healing sessions. They may pop in or you may call them in for some healing and telepathic communication. Remember that you and your guides are in charge here, so even if you need to confront old Uncle Pervert and his lecherous ways during your adolescence, you are 100 percent safe and in charge.

We suggest you take a deep breath and start finding out why your visitors are in your Akashic records. With the help of your guides and your soul family, you can connect their presence with what's going on in your life right now. More than likely your visitors' appearance is the help you've been asking for as you puzzle through a problem.

Family, Friends, Ancestors, and Loved Ones

You will find that your family, friends from all ages, and even your ancestors pop up and either challenge or support your healing process. Seeing a holographic image of these people is not the same as a soul part; what you are working with here is a memory, emotional habit, or message. This may also be a message that you have an unhealthy connection to them that needs a bit of attention; contracts, hooks, and drains may be brought to your attention this way, too (see chapter 11). Ask lots of questions when you see a person in your records. Since they are a representation of the energy that is around you, they are eager to share with you the reason why they are here. They are the best tattletale tellers ever.

✒ A Tip from Aunt Patty

Sometimes I just don't listen in real time. Here is how that was corrected in my Akashic records. On one visit to my record room I found Jacki hanging out waiting for me to arrive. My first reaction was, "Oh, now what?" I worried that I had screwed up something and she was going to tell me about it. (See how your complexes can cause you to jump to conclusions?) I was in for a big surprise. Jacki was there to give me a message, and that helped me to upgrade my perspective on our relationship.

I am nine years older than Jacki (there, I said it) and have been big sister and mommy to her for a very long time. Years ago that was very appropriate for us to nurture that kind of camaraderie, but now, as grown-ups and equals, I had not shifted my viewpoint to treat her as an equal adult. I was still seeing Jacki as the little sister I needed to take care of.

In a very loving and gentle way, Jacki's hologram told me, "Thank you for looking out for me, but I need you to let me be responsible for my own life." But what I heard was, "Hey Patty, I got this. You can go and focus on your own life now." I was floored. I hadn't realized that my helpfulness and nurturing were really me saying Jacki couldn't handle her own challenges and needed me to rescue her. I was energetically holding her back from developing self-confidence, and that was an important message for me to hear.

Ancestors in your records can be lovely, emotional reunions where they share with you that they are proud of you and happy, wherever they are. It's like your own mediumship moment! We say, if they came all this way for a cameo, ask them what else they want to share with you. Is there a hidden stash of cash in a wall somewhere? Some bearer bonds in the old family Bible? Maybe there is a gift or trait that they want to hand down to you, or maybe they want to warn you about a family curse or legacy. No matter what the message, when someone comes into your records there is always a gift, a healing, and a release, sometimes from things you never thought about before.

Immediate family and friends will pop in for a visit from time to time, too. Oh, and don't be alarmed if they are still among the living. You don't have to be a ghost to be a hologram. Follow their lead and see where they take you—usually to another part of your healing—and watch as they dissipate as your work is done. The best way to interact with these mirages is to be curious and ask questions.

The Legacy—Family Curses and Other Questionable Behaviors

Just as your DNA is passed through from one generation to the next, you inherit spiritual traits as well. We call these passed down traits your legacy, and it is the official pattern you inherit from your ancestors, both the good genes and the bad habits.

First, the good news. Legacies can be filled with gifts and talents. We choose to be born into our family for many good reasons, too. We pick them so we can have access to heroic qualities, talents, skills, social placement, wealth, love, support, and the opportunity to develop our soul through overcoming challenges. This is where the legacy comes into play.

In the planning of our next incarnation we set up circumstances for us to experience. If we want to continue to master a certain skill, we can take full advantage of the family tree. For example, choosing to be born into a family of talented musicians can be very instrumental in furthering our desire to master music ourselves. This seems like a simple scenario, and we wonder why we don't do this every time we plan out our upcoming life. Here's the rub: We may feel that success through struggle is what will make the mastery even sweeter. This is when the legacy shows its double-edged sword and the gift comes at a price. How we get around that is to choose to not participate in the part of the legacy that doesn't fit our paradigm. It's that simple.

Some other traits are learned, and some are like family curses or even contracts with entities or thought forms and beliefs that persist through the ages. Thank goodness you don't have to be stuck with them! Within your Akashic records you have the tools to find and fix any unwanted traits; not only for yourself, but for every family member present and past who wants to be rid of that energetic stain. But first you have to find your legacy and understand the story.

To uncover your own family legacies, start questioning things that you take for granted within your family, for example the things that are said during holiday get-togethers. Look for ideas that repeat: "our family doesn't do emotions," "alcoholism runs in our family," "that's the Batsford luck." Also look for things that may be silently repeated, like everyone being overweight, or having the same hereditary health problems. How about when a vast majority of the family has similar educational levels or careers? Even addictions can be a legacy. If you are often hearing, "You are just like your Uncle so and so," you may be staring a legacy right in the face. If you find yourself fearing that you'll grow up to be just like one of your parents, you fear a legacy is in place.

We can work with the energy of the family tree to minimize the effects of a negative legacy or to bring out latent talent, gifts, and strengths such as confidence and organizational skills. You can go really far back into the tree or stay local and work to heal faux pas from your parents' and grandparents' generations that are impacting you right now. Dipping in the wayback machine can help bring forward qualities that could have been bred out or lost through judgmental in-laws or social prejudices. If prissy Aunt Victoria turned her nose up at Aunt Annie Oakley on the family tree, you could be blocked energetically from the awesome qualities Annie could impart to you. Heck, you may just need them right now. Life is an adventure, and Annie may have just the right advice or attitude Auntie Victoria is clueless about.

Family Legacy in Action: A Story about Grandma T.

In our family we had this raucous gent named Kempf from Germany (Black Forest region). He was our grandmother's father on my dad's side. He had a handlebar mustache and wore a floppy hat, his skin was leathery brown, and everyone called him "the gypsy." He came to the United States with his family and settled in Long Island, New York.

Grandpa Kempf was a brewer and never learned to speak English. He had a notorious reputation and scared all his children away (and he had plenty of children to scare). But his courage and tenacity to survive in this new country while keeping true to his heritage were inspiring.

His wife was a healer and the strength behind this immigrant family. We are also healers and find our great grandmother to be a wonderful spirit guide in the "old ways." She shows up once in awhile as a spirit guide to help us with messages and encouragement. Being spiritual healers is our legacy from great-grandma Kempf. Being tenacious is a gift from our grandpa Kempf.

When we started looking at the Kempf family legacies, there was some conflicting energy: a harsh grandfather and a healing grandmother. This created conflict in us and our own family; anger towards those closest to us but also a desire to heal them at the same time. (Or was it anger that they weren't healing?) We had some sorting out to do.

Our grandmother (Dad's mom) was so motivated to get away from her parents she put herself in a less-than-perfect marriage. We found ourselves doing the same thing in our first marriages. Here is a classic example of an unconscious legacy at work, which we could only see in hindsight by asking questions about our family history while in our Akashic records.

Thank goodness for great-grandmother's healing legacy, because it propelled both of us forward easily as healers as we embraced the spiritual world, once we found it. This way when we found another legacy on our father's father's side, we were able to clear it easily.

Our father's father's side was another bunch of rowdy boys, Scottish this time, who started their own business. Our grandfather took care of the entire family, and his brothers were quite agreeable to that. What the family legacy did is create a belief that the family business will never quite be enough and we will always struggle. There was a lot of waiting until a miracle happened by those boys, and they leaned on their brother for guidance. They lacked confidence in themselves and the world around them.

Once us twenty-first-century sisters found and cleared this, we were able to really buckle down, learn about how to run a successful business, and start doing so. It was like a veil had lifted and clarity moved in to stay.

✳

Now let's work on one of your legacies. Find it by doing the meditation below and then decide what you want to do with this legacy. Your choices are: You can embrace it and choose to bring it more fully into your consciousness, or you can remove this pattern completely by hacking that part of the tree right off, burn the limb to ashes, and scatter the ashes to the four corners of the earth, never to be heard from again.

Meditation: The Family Tree

First, take a few slow, deep breaths.

Relax your shoulders, take another breath. Relax your feet, take another breath. Relax your scalp.

Acknowledge your connection to the earth and acknowledge your connection to the Divine. This simple act connects you to the earth and the Divine, and brings those energies into your body, blending and expanding.

Settle into your body. Your nose is in your nose, your toes are in your toes, your spine is in your spine, and your spirit is in your body.

Let all expectations or worries about the healing journey you are about to take just fall off of you as you settle more firmly into your body, and your aura shrinks to form a comfortable cloak around you.

Bring your attention into the center of your heart chakra. Experience its lovely green light as you flow into it. In the center of that green light is the door to your Akashic records. Take note of how it looks as you are going through it. Allow yourself to flow right through your door and into your records; they are yours and you are always welcome there.

As you go into your room, you see a grand and amazing tree growing in the middle of the room. It's beautiful; it's different and diverse. You see that the center of the tree is you: your life, your passions, your dreams, your day-to-day experiences. As you walk around this tree, you see how immense it is, and you see that it is also your family tree. The branches are your relatives, parents, siblings. You see how other trees touch your tree as they are the children of your ancestors.

Then start to experience your roots—those are the ancestors that are even older. The ancestors that you may have never met or don't know their names. As you experience the energy of the entire tree, you feel that you are the trunk, your family spreads all around you, and your ancestors are deep in the roots. There is a lot of information all around and through this tree.

Call to the keeper of tradition and legacies, Metatron. He holds the knowledge that is within all of the branches of your family. Admire this tree with your guide.

Ask Metatron, "What are the things in my life that are affected by the legacy of my ancestors? What are the good things my ancestors have brought to me? What did I inherit from their hard work?"

The keeper of tradition answers you as you watch flowers on your tree bloom with this awakening. You see leaves bud, and you watch as the tree becomes fuller and stronger from the acknowledgment that you have inherited all of these things.

The picture of your life becomes clearer, and you become stronger. You can feel the support from all the ancestors who love you. Allow yourself to take a moment and bask in this.

Now turn to Metatron again and ask, "What legacies have I inherited that block me, stop me, or bring pain, dis-ease, or unrest into my life?"

These things show up on your tree like a parasite, a choking vine, mold, toxic moss, or mushrooms. With each new parasite you see you understand what the belief, thought form, or entity is all about. As you logically understand this, Metatron is protecting you from the intense emotions through the generations. You see this legacy, you name it, and then you follow it down through the roots of your tree, past the bones that are under the tree, through time, to the origin of the legacy. A generation, two, three, seven, all the way back to its origin.

You ask Metatron, "What can I do to clear this? What can be surrendered and released? Does my ancestor know what they did or perpetuated? Can they be healed? Can I be healed? Is there any-one else in my family who wants to let got of this and be healed?"

Metatron understands how you will heal and change this leg-acy. He begins to answer all of your questions, and together you clear the contracts.

Archangel Michael, your angelic protector, comes in now and takes authority over any entity or thought form and clears it from your family tree.

You surrender and release these energies that no longer serve your family. You let them go with the Divine for whatever they need to do, and your tree gets stronger, you roots grow deeper, and you become stronger.

Invite the light, the sun, to shine on your family tree, illuminat-ing it all the way down to the roots and burning off any remaining toxins or harmful energy.

Watch as the history of your family changes. Watch as your records shift , as the vine, the parasite, dissipates. If any branches or roots cannot be healed, they can be cut off. You can even choose to plant a new tree for your new family.

Ask the keepers of tradition if there is anything else you need to know, anything else you need to see. Knowing that there will be more to look at during a later healing session, ask if there is anything pressing that must be addressed in this session.

Once you have finished, come back into the room and bring all that knowledge with you, keeping it in your resident memory. Write your experience and insights down in your journal.

Inner Enemies, Bogeymen, Aliens, Thought Forms, and Entities

We ask you many times in this book to check for thought forms and entities when clearing a contract, legacy, fear, etc. This is Jacki and Patty code for any sabotaging energy that will hang on to or recreate your issue once your back is turned. Though some are of your creation and some are foreign to you, we consider these energies together because you deal with them the same way. Really, it doesn't matter the origin; you invited them in and agreed to their influence at a spiritual and unconscious level. That's how these sabotaging energies work; they get in while you are vulnerable. They are tricky at the outset, but once they are outed for what they are, their power crumbles away. Once the scary crumbles, you are left with a messenger from your spirit to your consciousness.

It's easier to accept messages when you are relaxed and can suspend your judgment of the messenger and the situation from which they come. This especially applies when people show up who you have had serious challenges with or who are just downright frightening. Here we're referring to enemies, entities like the bogeyman and aliens. OK, you can include exes and evil bosses here, too. Your touchstone needs to be that (1) they are not real, and therefore cannot hurt you, and (2) it really is all about you, so Spirit is using a particular nemesis to teach you about your own shortsightedness, whatever that may be.

A Tip from Aunt Patty

I spent a lot of time being chased by aliens in my Akashic record room. I felt like I was on the Syfy channel every time they showed up. I honestly considered writing science fiction for a while. Since it is nearly impossible to validate the existence of aliens in my life or past lives even, I decided to let those little green men be metaphors for another kind of message. This brought more than a little sanity to me on this particular leg of the journey. It became pretty clear to me that I was feeling like a stranger in my own life (this was a spiritual habit for me). I never quite felt at home, anywhere, so I never really fully engaged in life. When you always feel like an alien or outsider where "nobody *under-staaaaands* me," you don't ever feel accepted, and that is a very lonely feeling. Spirit was showing me that I was the alien, and only I can fix that. I guess I was looking in the mirror the whole time. Ever since I started putting up a lot of resistance to creating intimacy with people and places, I started alienating myself from just about everything. Sure I had good reasons at the time, but I didn't have good reasons to continue being the odd man out anymore. Bottom line, it was up to me to make the first move and claim my life, my country, and my planet. My new spiritual habit was to practice grounding. This really helped me feel safer, enjoy my life, and let people get close to me emotionally. You love me, you really, really love me!

Bogeymen are here to give you the much-needed insight that is going to shine light on those dark corners in your mind. Bogeymen, evildoers, entities, even bugs demonstrate the power you have given away and challenge you to come and get it back. Go on, they dare you. Some of these characters hold in place the contracts you have taken on, others are there to show you what you are afraid of.

The act of will it takes for you to overcome your demons is exactly what is required of you to get your power back as well as your backbone. Doing this kind of sparring in your Akashic records is like training for real life. Not only are you facing your demons, you are releasing a ton of negative self-talk and toxic energy. Next thing you know you'll be ready to stand up for yourself in the flesh-and-blood world. This is a great example of how to create new spiritual habits that will shift your reality. One day the bullies in your life will realize you've become a contender. That is the day the scales tip in your favor.

Clearing the Saboteur

You may find that little minion of sabotage all on its own, or within other Akashic work you are doing. We are very good at putting in many layers that need to be cleared, so always peek under the rug to see if there is an inner enemy, entity, thought form, alien, or general bogeyman lurking. When you see it, put it under the spotlight of divine energy and ask Archangel Michael to take authority over it while you interrogate it for the last time.

Ask what it is, where it is from, and what its message to you is. Remember that it is fighting to keep its place in your Akasha, so get your truth meter ready to test its answers. Ask why it's sabotaging you and what it is getting out of this relationship with you. Why is it attacking this particular issue? Why does it want you to fail? Ask yourself what your reward is if you do fail. What agreement does this entity have with your ego? You may discover this saboteur is left over from an old agreement that you cleared or moved past in your waking life, and it is just echoing it.

Ask the aeons to gather any booby traps or backup systems that were put in place by this saboteur and then repair anything that was damaged by it.

You are now ready for Archangel Michael to take away the saboteur, all its baggage, and anything that was created by it. Once it is gone, look around. Does anything need to be detoxed, repaired, fixed? Call to the goddess Brigid to remove the leftover toxins, and ask your keepers to bring in the triage repair team to fix what your saboteur broke.

Now ask Haniel to fill in this void left by the saboteur with your energy combined with divine and earthly energy. Within this new divine energy you will find a gift that helps you create a new spiritual habit to replace the one your saboteur taught you.

Demons: Taking the Evil Out of Them

Demons are a step beyond entities. It seems like demons are really keyed into all of your weaknesses, your ego, and your fears, and they take advantage of them on every level possible. We took them out of the saboteur category because they can really scare you when you find them, and we deal with them a little differently. We are here to tell you don't be too scared of demons—they are total cowards.

In our recent study of the archangels and the Kabbalah we have been taught that demons are usually of our own making. They are made up of our negative actions, and they feed off of our fears, depression, and quest for power. Demons don't go where there is light because that is where they get really burnt (to a crisp even!). It was very validating, hearing this come from three thousand–year-old teachings, since we were already approaching demons in this way in the Akasha.

In Jacki's world the scariest movies are the ones that deal with evil spirits and demons. They really freak her out because she has met some in her Akashic journeys. Now, Hollywood does a great job making them scarier than they really are, but that still gets Jacki's scare factor going every time. The demons that you meet on your Akashic street may look as scary as the movie version, but when you put the light of the Divine on them, they run away. The job of a demon in your records is to get you to turn away from the Divine so they can feed off of your out-of-balance ego. Simple as that! They love negativity, they love depression, and they love to start energetic wars with other people through you. They are troublemakers to the end, but remember that they run away quickly when they are found out, leaving you to clean up the mess they left behind.

Yes, you want them gone. But if you don't understand why they are there and clear them out formally, they will creep back in and start the ruckus all over again. Archangels Michael, Ratziel, and Raphael are the demon fighters, and they always win. When you call on one or all of these archangels, they will take authority over the demon and clear it out without any extra effort on your part.

When you find a demon in your records, you have to get honest on your intentions and actions in the waking world. When you find a demon, you have some atonement to do of your own because demons feed off of negative actions. If you didn't have any negative actions, they wouldn't be there; don't start none, won't be none! For the most part no one likes to be the bad guy, we all feel our actions are justified and how dare the rest of the world not understand that! Yes, you are the bad guy sometimes, and until you can be honest with yourself about it, you will carry that demon with you and it will cause lots of havoc. When you are ready to confess and embrace the light, the demon can no longer reside within you.

We are not demonologists and we are not here to debate the presence of them in the waking world, we are only addressing the ones you find in your records. What we know and have experienced to be true is that taking the scary out of demons takes away their power to hurt you. Demons are easier to clear than entities, as long as you are willing to face the hard truths.

Clearing a Demon from Your Akashic Records

The first step in clearing a demon is to not panic. In fact, take it a step further: laugh at them. They worked really hard to look scary, and when you start to laugh at their ridiculousness, they pout a little, which in turn makes them even funnier. The big baby gorilla face is epic!

The second step is to call in archangel warriors; any and all. In a panic we all default to Michael, and Ratziel, but Raphael is well-suited for the job as well. Don't worry, whomever you call will bring in the right angel for the job. Ask your archangel to take complete and total authority over this demon and all of its toxins and damage.

The third step is to ask the demon why it is here. What action, behavior, or event attracted it in the first place? And why is it still here? The demon will try and lie to you, but those lies won't ring true, and hearing them may actually help you remember and take responsibility for your actions. The demon will tell you that it is there because of the actions of others. Liar! It may be the accumulated actions of you and others, but you signed up for this dance card, and you are tangoing with the best of them.

The fourth step is to take responsibility for yourself and your actions, without excuse or defense. No "ya, buts" allowed here; that phrase is demon food. Confess, admit, and ask your guide how you need to atone for this.

As soon as you are willing to atone for your actions and make amends, the demon is no longer able to stay around. Taking responsibility for your behavior and choices lets the Divine Light into the dark area of your soul and that demon is evicted!

The fifth step in clearing a demon is to invite the Divine Light into all areas of your life and all of your actions. You can't always make amends in the waking world, but you can take action in the Akasha to clear that energy out. In the waking world you have the option of a new behavior and attitude. If you choose the new one, that demon can no longer take hold in your life.

Superheroes and Saviors

When things are really out of whack, you may have to use extreme force to pull up and out of the imbalance. Just like a pendulum needs all its momentum to get to the other side of its swing, you too may need to call upon your inner superhero to knock the snot out of your bogeyman to move out of your negative beliefs or behaviors. Your Akashic superhero (tights and all!) is also your path to righteousness and your moral compass. He comes to your Akashic records to show you how it's done and gives you a boost of validation if you need to morph into a big green He-Man to accomplish your task.

Everyone needs a good guy when the chips are down. When you are dealing with the really hard stuff, you start to feel like you have screwed your life up and there will always be more crap waiting at every turn. Sometimes it just gets to be too much. We know how it is; we have had crises not only in our own Akashic sessions, but we have watched clients get there as well. Don't worry, our guides are happy to step in and give us the hero that we need.

If you are into comic books and sci-fi, Spirit will present you with the perfect hero for you to connect to and feel empowered by. Your superhero or savior may also be one of the divine allies you already work with: angels, ascended masters, gods, goddesses. You may get a visit from someone who lived an extraordinary life, like Gandhi or Abraham Lincoln. No matter what image you see, your hero is there to show you that you have what it takes to be a hero in your own right. Once that crisis is over, you will find that your superhero unmasked is you.

What did we learn from all of our discussion on soul swapping and spiritual bad guys? Anyone? Bueller? Ok, here's the gist. We are all functioning in a vacillating state of panic and believing we need rescuing more often than not. This is the biggest reason soul parts run amok and demons and inner saboteurs have jobs. The best way for you to not get overwhelmed with soul parts and bad guys is to pay attention to your relationships, including the relationship you have with yourself. Soul part swapping happens when people are worried about losing control. They use their soul part-charged agendas to turn the tides in their favor, so pay attention and keep cleaning house. Demons and saboteurs are all about making sure we live in doubt and fear. How else are they going to get us dependent on them? Get strong, know who you are, and challenge your demons often (and be sure to invite your angelic bodyguard along).

Chapter 11

The Promises We Make: Contracts, Curses, Hooks, Drains, and General Mayhem

Contracts are the glue that holds every issue tight to your records. Just when we think we are over something, it pops back up again, probably because there is a contract, vow, or curse acting like rubber cement and bouncing it right back in place. As you travel through these issues and short circuits in your records, take one more peek to see if there is a contract that started the ball rolling on that energetic pattern.

Contracts, vows, and curses are about making promises. We make promises to ourselves, to others, and to situations. Some vows or contracts are a beautiful statement of our love and commitment to another person, a lifestyle, or a personal philosophy. These promises help to remind us of our goals and help us keep on the path we've chosen. Many times two wedded people choose to renew their vows because it feels right and beautiful to rededicate their lives to each other.

We all remember the famous line from *Gone with the Wind* when Scarlett raised her fist and vowed, "As God is my witness, as God is my witness they're not going to lick me. I'm going to live through this and when it's all over, I'll never be hungry again. No, nor any of my folk. If I have to lie, steal, cheat or kill. As God is my witness, I'll never be hungry again!"

This is the kind of thing that seems like the right thing to do or say at the time, and it carries a boatload of conviction and passion, but it doesn't always stand up to the test of time. A vow to never go hungry again, and to lie, cheat, and steal to make sure it doesn't happen, can cause trouble in the future. Let's look at Scarlett's situation. Her broad statement of not wanting to ever feel hungry again was also about never being poor again. This vow guided her to be very creative in solving her problems and to recreate her life on her terms, but not always necessarily to her betterment. This is how a vow or contract can help you overcome a weakness and support you on your way to self-sufficiency. Where a declaration of this kind causes an issue is when it continues to feed our fear of lack or is used to remind us only of the pain and misery we vowed to overcome. In the poverty scenario, we could end up obsessing about food and have overstocked kitchens, cook large meals for two, waste food, become a shopaholic, or feel anxiety and overeat. Food can then become our balm as we use it to soothe anxious feelings of any kind.

We've all had our Scarlett O'Hara moments and have made a private promise to never have that painful experience happen again. This is called shoring up and creating resolve, and it takes will and a decision or choice. The unfortunate part is that we often match the intensity of the promise to the intensity of the situation and our feelings around it. That is why contracts, promises, vows, and curses use a lot of dramatic language like "never," "always," and "forever." This kind of inflexibility eventually comes back to haunt us. When that happens, we can go into our Akashic records and rewrite or cancel the contracts.

Vows kept are not the issue; it is the ones we make that are not kept that can cause the proverbial car crash in our lives. When we cannot fulfill a vow made, it is time to go into the records to change the past and un-promise what is now creating a disturbance in our force.

Contracts: Sign on the Dotted Line Please, Never Mind the Fine Print

Let's get some definitions straight here. Contracts are binding agreements we make to ourselves or another to uphold a behavior, situation, or belief. We go into a spiritual contract with someone to help us create something, keep us from doing something, or take responsibility for us. We create contracts around a belief because we feel so strongly about a truth or perspective that we need to embody it. These kinds of contracts often are a result of a traumatic event, or come right down the family tree from our parents and ancestors, and we agree to it as part of our heritage.

Looking at contracts from a soul's perspective, we find that we use them to mold the general direction of our experiences so we can learn to overcome challenges that bring depth and wisdom to us. If we are looking to learn about our self-worth, we can use the lessons of poverty to teach us that facet. Other times we'll use relationships with other people to teach us about our worth. It's the contract that keeps the energy in place until we have figured the lesson out and can move past the pattern. Unfortunately, when we are done with that lesson, the contract is still in place, keeping us bound to the agreement we made.

When we find a contract in our records, we can look at it and decide if it still serves us and then make changes. It's all our choice. Life can be the best barometer to the relevance of a contract. An old, worn-out contract hanging around in our records will muck up our progress because it's energetically enforcing an old agreement. (No wonder that airtight plan for success keeps blowing up in your face.) The good news is, when we make the changes to our contracts in the Akashic records, it will change the way our life unfolds from there.

Contracts also come with an energetic pattern that keeps us from straying too far from it. This energy pattern or entity is sometimes seen as something scary, like a bogeyman or demon, and it does its best to scare us into compliance. It works just about every time. For those of us who are not easily scared, our entities will be more like locks, or booby traps that will go off when the right wire is tripped. These are more for the MacGyver or Houdini types. Everyone has their own ways of sabotaging their progress, and that is what the entity is for. So be forewarned. They are more than an alarm; they're independent, self-motivated, thinking, calculating beings with their own agenda here. You've basically hired a bouncer to keep you in line.

Soul Contracts: And They Call Me a Capitalist! Harrumph

Every good contract in business is written to be mutually beneficial for each party and has closure. We go into contract with people because we require help in some way and we've found someone who has the skills or resources we need. The contract in and of itself is not the issue, but why we've gone into contract and the terms of that contract can be problematic.

Oy, the emotional contracts we get into! They are not as clean, and we can sometimes find ourselves in situations that are more damaging than helpful, with no foreseeable way out. When we make agreements under duress, we are often looking for a rescue or bailout. Believe you me, there are no shortages of people looking to take advantage of us based on their own needs, wants, and desires. (Can you say agenda?)

Even parents go into contracts with their children. Ever see a family where the child has taken care of their able-bodied parent throughout their childhood and beyond? This is a classic contract between two souls where value, respect, and individuality are not honored. The adult child's healing path will include developing independence and self-respect while the parent will have to learn to accept that their child is not an extension of themselves and should be seen as a person with a unique destiny in life. Each party has their own lessons to learn, and going into contract with one other can stimulate that understanding and maturing, but it will be a harsh learning curve for both. If you find this describes your life to a T, we recommend getting professional help with this powerful lesson and teacher. When you look at this contract in the Akashic records, you will get the unique message of the relationship and the understanding on how to rewrite it.

Discovering that there is a contractual reason for the difficult circumstances in a relationship is the key to unlocking and freeing the soul parts and making real changes in the way you interact with someone. Learning the terms of the contract will always point you toward yourself. All contracts are symbiotic, meaning that even though you might feel used, you are still getting something out of this relationship. Bottom line, it's all about you: what you needed, what you were sacrificing, what you agreed to, how you used the other person, why you needed to give yourself away or not be yourself, and finally, what you learned about yourself through this experience.

Contracts can give us a feeling of futility, and we think that breaking them will be as difficult as living them. This is not the case. Breaking an emotional contract is as easy as changing your mind. Most of the time when we find a broken soul part made the contract, we have already learned the lion's share of the lesson. We have already questioned the validity of this agreement, and it's a good sign that the contract is hanging by a thread. We have come to see ourselves in a better light.

Social Contracts

Some contracts we are born with; contracts that are socially based like issues with our race, sex, sexual orientation, the neighborhood we live in, and many other social norms. For example, saying the pledge of allegiance as a child created a contract between you and America. This may be a contract you love and are proud of and consider to be in alignment with who you are. In our Akashic Wisdom Process we are only advocating clearing contracts that no longer help you reach your goals.

These different social norms get so much energy from the people contracted to them that they start to become energetic all on their own; entities, as it were. Think about it—women have the contract to be caretakers, and men have the contract to become the providers. We are born into this, but we can choose to be something different than this societal norm. Being skinny or fat gets a contract too, and there are entities in the Akasha who hold those contracts. They are usually connected to your Akashic records by the issues that are triggered by the contract. We have found contracts that create opinions and beliefs about one's race, where you live, and most assuredly what religion you were born into and committed to.

🖊 A Note from Aunt Jacki

As I write this I am remembering a time when I cleared a contract with the entity that is America. After that, I stopped saying the pledge of allegiance in any venue. I get grief about it, as if I am not a true American. I say that I am such a true American I use my rights of free speech not to speak at times.

Contracts Are Like Pie Crusts: Easily Made and Easily Broken

We work with archangels to break or rewrite contracts. Our favorites are Michael and Gabriel for contracts that are of this lifetime. Michael is great overall for contracts, but especially good on societal contracts and anything to do with protection. Gabriel is excellent at rewriting contracts, as he has a way with words. Archangel Tzaphkiel is on tap for those contracts that carried through from a past life. Archangel Khamael is very helpful for contracts that involve a partnership, either business or one with someone you love very much. We look to the archangels to help us understand the fine print and whether or not the agreement still fits us. They help us find a way out of the contract by clearing it outright, taking us back in time and helping us unmake it, or coming up with the perfect rewrite.

Rewriting a contract is not re-engaging the other party; it is taking the contract to a higher healing level with ourselves and the Divine, and a rewrite always has an expiration date. The purpose of rewriting a contract is to help us hold the new healing energy within our records and within ourselves until this new energy pattern has taken hold.

Clearing a Contract (This Time Read the Fine Print)

In life every good business contract is written to describe the scope of the agreement, and it has closure, too. We go into contract with people because we need help in some way, and we've found someone who has the skills or resources we need. This is not the kind of contractual agreement we are talking about in the Akashic records. These silent energetic contracts you make (like your life depended on it) are rarely beneficial and usually quite one-sided. Basically, no attorney worth their salt would agree to half the contracts you've entered into.

When we are working in the records and we bring up an issue, the first thing we ask is: Are there any contracts? We know that this is where a dose of self-honesty is in order. With any issue we find in our records we have to ask what the reward for the pain we are experiencing is. Many times underneath all that drama we will find the contract that keeps the gerbil wheel spinning. The reason for the original agreement may have become distorted over time, but it holds the contract in place and keeps you energetically connected with a dissonance that is affecting your waking life. No matter what the issue that is being addressed, ask these tough questions:

* "What did I agree to?"
* "How am I using this contract?"
* "What am I getting out of this contract?"

It often takes more than personal willpower to break a contract; we need to understand why we created a contract in the first place. As with all deep healing, lessons need to be learned and behavior needs to change or we'll go right back and create a new contract to replace the old one. At this point the contract has become a security blanket.

Contracts take on so many forms in the Akashic records; from a legal brief to a ball and chain, ornate scroll, stone tablets, hang tags, really anything you relate to as a legal and binding document. Very old contracts may look old, while contracts with family members may show a face or something that reminds us of that person. There are many more symbols, and the ways they are presented are clues to how long this agreement has been in place and the circumstances in which it became binding.

Contracts also feel restricting, like having to sit in our desk after the school bell rings, or being stuck in rush-hour traffic. We can't wait to be done with the experience when we find a contract. This is exactly the reason why we look for contracts when we bring up an issue. Contracts can be the basis for frustration and anxiety, and the good news is, they can be broken.

If you find yourself antsy and ready to exit the records in the quickest way possible, slow your roll and take a moment to ask if this is a contract.

Just for fun and practice, go into your records to see if there are any contracts ready to be released so you can experience their energy and be able to recognize them easily in the future.

When you feel you have come across a contract, these few steps will get you through the healing fairly quickly.

1. Ask the Archangel Gabriel to help you get a visual or an understanding of the contract.

2. Ask Gabriel to take authority over the contract so you can relax and focus on it.

3. Ask who the contract is with and why. Let the story unfold; put it up on the screen if you need to watch how the movie plays out.

4. Ask for the bottom line on this contract. For example, "You will hire crazy people or make your employees crazy because you asked for an exciting work environment," or "Your mother has contracted with you to always criticize you to keep your ego in check," or "Your house doesn't want you to leave." (That last one was a true story.) Once you have the story behind the contract, you can do your Akashic magic.

5. Ask if this contract can be cleared, or if it needs to be rewritten. If it is to be rewritten, ask why and ask for the new words. Don't forget to include an exit clause and an expiration date.

6. Ask for all discomfort caused by this contract to be cleared and for the new version to bring you blessings, balance, and Divine Light.

7. When you have a contract ready to be cleared, you have to make sure you get all the junk that goes with it. Repeat this request to make your intention clear.

> Archangel Gabriel,
>
> Please take complete and total authority over this contract of (insert information here). Clear all its connections, entities, booby traps, and bombs. Delete this contract from my Akashic records, all lifetimes, dimensions, and past and future generations. Clear this out of every layer of my aura and my memory, and remove any spiritual habits that may have resulted from this contract.

8. Add anything else we may have missed in that list. You want to make sure you get every last drop.

9. One final step in clearing contracts is to identify and change the behavior. Whatever you did as a result of this contract needs to be let go of and changed. Before you leave your Akashic records, ask to be shown the new behavior you need to do to support your new attitude. Make sure to write a new affirmation, too.

Vows: As God As My Witness . . .

As soon as we are old enough to reason, we start making vows. Vows are promises you have made to yourself or to another. It is as simple and as powerful as that. Vows are different from contracts in that they are personal promises and do not have entities attached to them. A vow can be inspired by something we believe in, so when breaking a vow, look for the belief that inspired it. Each vow is personal and circumstantial and rarely hereditary, but we can make a vow to try and avoid a family habit or pattern from taking root in our life.

When you make a vow to another, like a marriage vow, you are blending your lives and energy together not only in your waking life, but in your Akashic records too. There are also vows you make to yourself to help you change your behavior or make a course correction of your life circumstances. We even make vows to prevent something from happening in the future. We often layer our vows, because previous vows long forgotten about are already influencing our life.

Vows are powerful because all the energy of them is in the making of them. Think about all the emotions felt in a wedding ceremony when the couple takes their vows: not a dry eye in the house. Think about the absolute commitment you feel at midnight, before you go to sleep, that you are going to wake up the next morning to work out and will start that new diet. Even better still, the vow you make to a loved one to never disrespect or hurt them again. The power lies in the making of them, leaving nothing for you to use in carrying them out. Vows fulfilled are not the issue; it is vows that are broken or made with the wrong intention that cause the disturbance and short circuit. Broken vows hang out in your Akashic records and cause havoc, guilt, anger, frustration, and limitation. They stand between you and what you really want to manifest. They take up that space that would be better filled with divine blessings that actually get you closer to your end goal (a.k.a., working in cooperation with the Divine).

Not all broken vows get stuck. Within your waking life you do things that create healing in your Akashic records; therapy, making amends, talking out the tough stuff with friends, and taking responsibility for yourself. What you can find in your records are shells of vows that are waiting to be re-energized or just cleared away to have new habits put in their place.

Clearing a Vow

When you find a vow, it feels a bit guilty, remorseful, or restrictive, depending on the type of vow you are uncovering. It looks less like the binding document with another person as in a contract and more like a promise you made that stops you from moving forward in life. We will often find our vows in our records with a soul part connected to them. That soul part is desperately trying to fulfill the vow over and over again. A vow made under duress will have a little piece of us holding the memory of the event. Look for a soul part of the person you made the vow with also; you will need to clear all of it.

When you find a vow, your first course of action is to ask your keepers if you need to know what this vow is. History proves to us that 99 percent of the time your keepers will say, "Yes, you need to know the details on this." (That 1 percent of the time is when you discovered a vow in your waking life and are already working on it; either way you can't avoid the work.) Look for who the vow is with and when the vow was made.

When you find this vow, look for any other vows connected to it. Like all the times you vowed that you wouldn't eat chocolate cake anymore or drink that much, or that you would remember your anniversary. You may have layered similar types of vows to force a behavior change or hold on to an ideal of belief.

Connected to your vow may be a belief. This belief may simply be something you have outgrown and it's ready to be cleared, but it is connected with a vow. If that belief is deeply rooted, then refer to the section on clearing beliefs later in chapter 12. If the belief is stubborn, then that is a clue to you that your belief is holding on to the vow that you may have already worked on releasing, and the belief needs your focus before you address the vow.

Soul parts are notorious for sticking to vows that you have made to yourself. That vow to go to the gym has a soul part that continues to pump iron. Ironically, that soul part can actually stop you from fulfilling your vow. It is doing all the work already, so your desire to hit the gym is fulfilled by it. Call to Archangel Tzaphkiel to gently remove that soul part from the vow to cleanse it of the job it had been doing in fulfillment of it. Tzaphkiel will ask you if you want this cleansed soul part back to fill in the place where your vow will be removed from. Sometimes the damage to a soul part is too severe and they just want to go back home. For a deeper healing with this soul part refer to the soul part section in this chapter.

Ask Tzaphkiel to help identify if there are any soul parts that do not belong to you attached to this vow. If there are, ask Lilith or Kwan Yin to take authority over these soul parts and return them to their owner. Also ask them to bring back any of your parts that may be stuck with the other person. Ask them to cleanse your soul parts before they are returned to you.

You have released the belief and the soul parts, making it time to travel back to the moment where you created that vow, or the first vow in your layers of vows. Your Akashic records may change form to look like that moment where you made the vow, it may put you in the wayback machine, it may put a movie up on the wall, but once you are ready, you must go back to that moment and rewrite it.

Rewriting your vow is easy; you just make a different decision or change the words coming out of your mouth. Avoid any words like "promise" or "I swear." Those are all vow-creating words. Use phrases like "it is my intent," "I want," or "I will work towards." If you are dealing with a moment of duress or desperation when that vow was made, then pray. Pray for strength and focus, or divine intercession, or the fortitude to do whatever it is you were about to cast a vow upon.

Ask Tzaphkiel to help you see and change all the moments, all the decisions, and all the areas in your life that were affected by this vow. Ask your keepers to update your records. You are requesting that they take the vow out of your records. This will remove any triggers of sabotage that get activated when you do anything contrary to the vow you made and then broke.

All this moving and shaking in the records is about replacing the vow with a new statement that is healthy and empowering, and it cascades through all of your Akashic records and through your waking life. Now the real work starts: your homework.

Once you clear the vow and are ready to face the waking world, you have a new habit to create. You must take your new statement and start working it. You are now empowered to make new choices; do so. If you go back to your old behavior, you can undo much of what you healed because you aren't supporting it in your day-to-day.

Curses, Hexes, and Ill Intent, a.k.a. Put a Wart on It

Curses, jinxes, crossed conditions, hexes, evil eyes, bad mouthings, and overall malicious intent. When we think of these things, we think of someone casting them upon us and that we are doomed for many generations to come. Maybe you imagine an evildoer bent over a cauldron, casting your name into the pit of hell. It's rare that someone would take the time and trouble for all of that magical energy. This is a very old-fashioned idea, but it still puts us in a very frightened state of mind just thinking of it. What's more likely is that curses and negative intentions from others can and do make their way to you, and they hang out waiting for an opportunity to screw up your best, most foolproof plans.

So often, when a curse is found, we wonder, "what did I do to deserve this?!" It is tempting to throw it right back at the caster, but that doesn't solve anything. That keeps you tied to the curse, and it is still active in your Akashic records causing trouble. It is also tempting to freak out and lose your shit, but now is the time to "keep calm and carry on." You don't have to be afraid of this curse, it's just a bunch of energy with a negative instruction. You know how to deal with energy, and you have big-time backup when you are dealing with curses.

It always takes two to tango, and although you may not immediately know what you did, some digging will help you uncover what you or your ancestors did to invoke the rage of some powerful mojo. When you find a curse in your records, ask your keepers for the backstory on this situation so you may better understand how your actions affected the situation. The backstory will tell you a lot about why this curse happened, and if you ask correctly, it will tell you the story of the caster of the curse. There has to be a lot of spiritual pain within someone to throw so much negativity upon another that it becomes a curse. We know, you don't care about the other person since they cursed you so, but you may want to. You may want to care and learn the why so it doesn't happen again. In the cases of family curses that started generations ago that information is not as relevant as curses that were thrown upon you in this life.

For instance; a coworker wants the promotion as much as you do. Since you are both up for the promotion, there is competition as to who will get it. One day the boss is at your desk while you find a mistake that your coworker made. You fix it, look like the hero, and get the promotion. The promotion doesn't go so well for you. You make mistakes you never have in the past, you lose things, the boss is mad at you. You discover that the coworker cursed you.

Knowing why they cursed you is important because it tells you how to protect yourself in the future. You undo the curse, things go well, and you block that coworker from putting the whammy on you again. You can even look into the karmic relationship with them and seek forgiveness for how you hurt them in your records and reach some type of peace accord.

Another instance could be that you pissed off your best friend so much she blew an energetic gasket and you got the blast of it. Eventually you make up and resume the friendship, but you are still walking around with this negative energy that became a curse. There was really no evil intent, but an emotional outburst. You don't have to kill the friendship or even tell your friend about it, just clear it and know that your actions really triggered something in her and take care in the future.

You are not alone in figuring all this out; Archangel Raphael clears curses, and Archangel Khamael will help clear the relationship with the curse caster so it doesn't happen again. If this is a family curse, call to the ancestor whose actions triggered the curse and have the curse cleared from them, allowing it to be released from every generation after. St. Germain is another ally to call upon, as he will make sure all aspects of your life that are affected by the curse are cleared of its toxin.

Curse energy is dense, dark, and filled with strong negative emotions such as jealousy, hatred, or revenge. It can look like a black or dark streak in your aura or in your Akashic record room. When you find this energy, relax, settle into your space, and ask for the backstory. It may start to play on your screen, download into your memory, or be told to you by your guides. The reason you want to know the story is so you can get all sides and motivations. This will allow you to be more open to understanding others' perspectives and experiences. It will also help you get to that place of forgiveness so you can let it all go.

If you have a family curse that has caught your attention, take the attitude that you took this on because you are capable of dealing with it. We often chose to be born into a family so we can help with the karma backlog. Its like volunteering to clean out the family home to make it a more pleasant place to live. Some of the karma is our own and some of it belongs to others, and we can help our family balance their karmic debts. We are all here in service to each other. Isn't that fun!

This is how you can efficiently deal with a curse in your Akashic records.

Clearing a Curse

Please read this all the way through before launching your own curse removal meditation.

Once you are safely in your Akashic record room, identify that you have a curse that you need to clear and ask the archangels to confirm it is a curse. They will help you understand where it came from if necessary. Let the story become a memory or to play up on the screen. You might open a book and watch it take place among the pages, or look into a crystal ball like the Wicked Witch of the West.

Once you have the gist of the story, and you will probably only get the highlights and the key players, it's time to choose to step away from this reality. You will need to stop agreeing to carry this energy, forgive the source of the curse, and forgive yourself for the part you played in the whole drama.

Remember, curses happen because of anger between two people. Even if there is a huge misunderstanding—and there usually is. To break a curse you have to be willing to stop holding on to the pattern and let it go. You will be surprised at how trivial the conflict has become over time, or it doesn't matter anymore because everyone has been long gone. If the fight was over money or relationships, realize that the deeper issue is not about that at all, but really about feeling powerless to effect change in one's life. The drama between you and the other party is about taking fear to extremes and insisting that someone is to blame for one's own misery. As hard as this is to believe, you at some point agreed to being cursed. Sounds pretty silly, but that's the only way an energy pattern can stick to you. You have to believe it to be true. One way we do that is to feel unforgiving, guilty or sorry for the other person. That just leads us to take responsibility for someone else's lessons, and that never works.

Jumping forward to the place where you understand what you are letting go of, it's now time to break that pesky curse. Call upon Archangel Raphael to take a hold of the curse and break it, and ask that all the pent-up emotions, thoughts, and beliefs be drained from you as you let it all go. Once that is done, open up your crown chakra and pull in your light to fill you with your truth.

It's OK to ask for a gift from your guides to remind you of the new and improved you. It could be a tool, a color to add to your aura, a new guide, or something that represents the empowerment you've just embraced. You have healed an old belief you had about yourself, or the family believed about itself, and it's time to hold the vision of a stronger, more balanced you.

Another suggestion for those who love ritual is to choose a stone or crystal to dump all the nasty energy into by holding the stone over the area of your body that feels the most clogged with this energy. You'll know which one it is, it'll hurt. Pain is a great indicator of an energy block.

🖋 Warning

Pain is also an indicator of a physical issue. Don't assume anything, and see a doctor if you are not able to resolve your aches and pains via spiritual healing or meditations.

Once you feel all the icky, dense energy has released into the stone you can dispose of it in the earth or in running water. This is a fantastic way to cleanse the stone and recycle the energy. The earth is the best filter we've got. Note: don't bury the stone on the property you live on or flush it down your toilet. This ceremony will help your unconscious ground the energetic changes you have just made into its little reality engine. Your life will begin matching your dreams when your unconscious is on the same page with your consciousness. This is why it's so important to get the skeletons out of the closet. They may look dead, but they are not—and boy will they cause trouble when you try to move on with your life without them.

Hooks: Hookin' Ain't Just for Hookers

Hooks are an energetic barb with a line that attaches one person's aura to another. It looks like a fishing line and hook; that's why we call it a hook. When you get hooked, it can come on as a sneezing fit, or it may feel like you've just been stung or bitten by an insect. Occasionally it feels like a sudden muscle cramp. Hooking is a very physical thing, and the sensation is usually no more dramatic than that.

The emotional and mental drama associated with hooking will be more of a challenge. You will feel like you are being manipulated. You'll find you are changing your viewpoint and feelings on a subject and going against your own instincts and values. This vacillating is a pretty good sign that you've been hooked.

Someone might throw a hook in your direction because they really need to make themselves known to you. Their investment in getting you to understand them and agree with them is so strong that they need to energetically guide you and keep you under their influence.

Hooking into someone is usually done unconsciously, but still it is a willful behavior. We do it because we're afraid of losing someone's support. We do it because our ego can't stand not being in control, and when we are too insecure to allow other opinions in the room, the hooks start flying.

Hooks are not just the weapon of the loudmouths, either. More than likely it's the quiet ones you have to look out for. Those who feel powerless and have the hardest time with confrontation will be the first to throw out a hook in an attempt to level the playing field. Think of hooking as a way to communicate when something is really important to you but you are too afraid to speak up. Or, maybe you are ignored because you are soft spoken and timid. Quiet just means quiet, not stupid. The quiet ones are often very resourceful because they spend more time observing their surroundings and—*shazam!*—a brilliant idea for getting their point across materializes.

Don't get your ego in a twist and think you would never hook anyone and it is only done to you. The long and short of it all is, kids hook their parents, coworkers hook their bosses and other coworkers, friends hook friends, and leaders of communities hook their constituents. Nice people hook, mean people hook, tall people hook, short people hook, black, white, and green people hook. Essentially, everyone hooks those they need to persuade, sell their point of view to, or use to feed their ego. When hooking happens, somebody is not feeling heard and is resorting to covert activities.

✒ A Tip from Aunt Patty

If you are having a sneezing fit and tingling nose and you can't locate the source—there's no dust, herbs, or typical allergen—consider that someone is really needing your attention or cooperation. Take an inventory of the people in your life who you may have disagreed with, not have had time for, or have said no to recently. As you think of the person who has sent the hook, the area of attachment will react. The same applies for hooks that cause pinches, stings, or cramps.

When you are in your Akashic room and you see wisps and filaments coming from somewhere and attached to your body, you most likely have some folks who need you to be in their corner and they are not feeling acceptance or understanding from you. It is in your best interest to clear these energetic connections out of your aura. Hooks are not a substitute for conversation, and everyone needs to learn to cope with waiting their turn, differences of opinion, and that no means no. Conversely, we all need to learn to not let people manipulate us and that each and every one of us is a worthy and valuable person with a purpose for being here. When you allow hooks to stay in place, you are devaluing the meaning of your life and in essence hiding behind codependent behavior. At first it may seem like you are in service to another human being and that will feel very noble, but ultimately you will come to resent the way you are being treated and rebel. Save yourself the trouble and frustration and just say no to hooks!

Akashic Miracles from Aunt Jacki

I was looking at a curse in my records, and boy was I pissed that this person whom I had helped out greatly in the past had cursed me! How dare they! I calmed down and decided that before I cursed them right back, I would ask for the backstory. The backstory humbled me greatly. Yes, I had helped that person out greatly, but in my ignorance I had also hooked into them and tried to control their life. I didn't intend that, and I can see with how much drama was going on in their day-to-day, and how much I loved them, I was trying to control everything to make them happier. That may feel loving for a minute but quickly turns into feeling stifled and controlled. They took all their frustrations about me, balled it up, and pelted me with it in the form of a curse just to get me off their back.

My higher self got in contact with their higher self so I could remove my hooks and ask for forgiveness. The curse just melted away with no additional help. I am friends with this person again, and we have a new and healthy relationship.

Clearing a Hook

Once you have figured out who is responsible, you can begin to remove the hook. First, call upon your favorite guardian protector in spirit to help you. Archangel Michael and his flaming sword is always a good choice to disconnect the hooks for you.

In your imagination, push the hook out from the inside as your spirit guide pulls it from the outside. Now, you don't want these hooks going back like a retractable cord to the originator. If you do that they will know right away and then send out another batch to re-hook you. When energy ricochets back to a person, it feels like they are under attack (even though it's their own stuff), and they will react instinctively to dig in deeper with you.

Instead, ask Michael to replant those hooks into the earth or into the Divine so that the flow of energy is uninterrupted. No one is the wiser, and you have kept this unhooking under the other person's radar until a healthier relationship with them can be established (your next step). Alternatively, you can ask that the hook be dissolved. Stealth is the key here. The energy the hooker receives from this alternate unending source is healthier for them than your personal funk, and it will naturally dissolve once they have moved past this issue themselves.

Don't walk away, you aren't done yet! Here is where the real work comes in. Why was the hook there in the first place? Why did you agree to it? To find that, put your attention on the area where the hook was removed and look for the thing that it was anchored to.

Ask questions like: Is this a contract, a soul part, an inner child, a belief, a fear? Am I having guilty feelings? This shows how everything is connected and how you are in control of all that goes on in your world. You are the one with the magnet that drew the hook. If you clear that vulnerability, you won't have to do this (for this specific reason) ever again.

Once you get your question answered, then you know what your next step is, and you can flip to that part of this book (as opposed to your Akashic record book). If you get an answer you don't understand and that isn't in the book, be assured your guide is getting ready to teach you something new. It's time to ask lots of questions like: What do I do with this? What does it mean? Who will help me with this? Or, more likely, you will start with, "Get it off me!" and then ask those other questions.

You can then send a mental message to the hook sender that this is not the best way to communicate with you, and hooks are not acceptable. If the hook is sent from someone who is aggressive, intentionally wishing to manipulate you or control you, and not in a good space, you will need to take steps to protect yourself energetically. Hooks from people you normally have a loving relationship with need help developing healthier communication, and that requires attention from you, so figure out a way to facilitate that. Put down your resentment and take your turn being the grown-up.

If you are the person sending the hooks, stop it! Retract your hooks and ask those same questions you would ask if someone else's hooks were in you, as well as a few more for introspection: What are you trying to gain from this? What is your agenda? What are you not getting from this person, and how can you verbally ask for it? If you need help, call to Michael and he will be happy to help you and talk to you about what your lesson is here. Michael may be a beefcake warrior, but he is really smart too, with a lot of good things to tell you.

Drains: Dwain the Bathtub, I Am Dwowning!

As Madeline Kahn famously sang in *Blazing Saddles,* "I'm *so* tired . . . ain't it a freakin' shame." Just talking about energetic drains makes us tired. That is what drains do, they drain away things. Drains are used to siphon off and take vital energy from your aura and send it directly to the other person. They literally feel stronger, happier, more vital, and stable, and it can give them a real high. Think back to the last time you listened to someone's problems and they felt amazing afterward and you felt like you'd just been flogged and left to die. That, my friend, is a drain in action. Drains can happen over the phone, IM, and email too, because energetic links are made through electronics and through thought. Someone can focus on you intently and make a drain connection.

We can create and attach a drain to another's aura just like we can with a hook. It's a fascinating phenomenon, but it can make you feel like you've suddenly come down with the flu or your pancreas just stopped metabolizing sugar. Like a spirit possession, a psychic drain feels very nasty and sudden. It will give you a headache, make you sick to your stomach, make you dizzy, and give you hot flashes, cold sweats, shaky hands, brain fog, and blurry vision, to name the most common sensations. Yuck.

Drains that have been there a long time (within this lifetime) can cause long-term illnesses, listlessness, depression, and general bad luck. Drains are like hooks on steroids. People can drain you of your energy or reverse drain their funk into you for many reasons. Mostly it's because they see you as the life raft during their personal perfect storm, or their dumping ground for all their toxic waste they can't stomach any longer. Poor babies, they really are feeling overwhelmed and need rescuing, but they don't know how to ask for help. This is not new. We've been sucking each other dry for generations, and it's time now to stop the draining madness and learn a better, more mature way of dealing with our problems.

Job one is to recognize draining is going on, and then stop it and remove it. Remember, it takes two. An agreement that has some benefit for you allows a drain to continue to exist, so take responsibility for your role in this and work directly with the removal of the drain. Contracts or vows are very often connected to drains, especially if they have been there for a long time. You have to look at what your pain or reward was for this drain. What did you get out of the agreement to put this drain in place? It is more important to find your end of the drain partnership than the antagonist's reason. You can try to change the other person, but you can change yourself so much more quickly and easily.

Very few people will remove the drains they send out to you. They probably don't even recognize they are doing it. All the lecturing and caretaking of the other person will not change the fact that they are draining you; it will just make you look a little cuckoo. The drainer is just not in a place to be able to hear you or respond in a healthy way because they are at their weakest and most desperate point. They are getting what they need from you, and there is no motivation to change. Frankly, this is way beyond a call for help; they have decided to abdicate their problems to you. Lucky you! They must really love and trust you because you are so loving and strong and wise and will know what to do for them.

Wrong. Period. Even though most drains are unconscious, the one who is doing the draining is not loving and trusting to you in a healthy way. They are totally using you. They haven't a care in the world who you are and if you can handle it. If you even try to give them advice or help them learn to be responsible for themselves, they will probably come at you like a rabid dog. Sorry, it's the way it is. When we are so ill that we have resorted to draining someone, we are pretty far gone. We just want someone to take care of our issues for us so we don't have to feel it, look at it, and deal with it. It's kind of like trying to save a drowning person and they take you down with them. To make things even more interesting, they may have even convinced themselves that you are the cause of their pain and they are just giving back to you what you deserve. It gets complicated, and it's best to focus on taking care of yourself and be as neutral as you can toward the person who has sent you the drain. Here's the kicker: you agreed in some way, on some level, that it's OK that this person drains you, so once you remove it, you are that much more empowered.

Getting the drains off is easier and more straightforward than making sure it never happens again. Relationships where there are hooks and drains have a history of established habits and behaviors on both ends of the drain. Undoing those patterns is part of the long-term healing process that we all go through our entire life. Not many people can overcome this kind of challenge without help, and that is why there are healers of all kinds walking the face of the earth. If you have poor boundaries and a lot of codependency going on, find yourself a good therapist and spiritual healer to help you on this part of your journey.

Don't forget about the reverse drain, also known as dumping. Lord help you if you have a reverse drain. Ever have the sewer back up into your basement? Oh the horror! Get the hazmat suit on and make sure your shots are up to date. Here your needy friend or family member can't cope with everything that is going wrong with their life and needs a place to offload excess toxicity. This will include negative emotions. You know the ones—anger, jealousy, hatred, fear, and self-loathing. Of course there are more, but let's also talk about the damaged soul parts that get dumped, too. These are little fragments of themselves that hold the pain and anguish from any event that caused trauma, feelings of failure, and disappointment. They don't know what to do to heal these little guys, and they are tired of listening to them, so off they go down the drain to your house. Ahhhh, you're just a flush away from nirvana, so find this connection and get it the hell out of there!

✒ Akashic Tales from Aunt Jacki

I had a contract a long time ago to allow all my employees to reverse drain to me so they could focus on their jobs. This was created during one of our busiest seasons in our busiest year, and I needed each and every one of them on their game. For some reason, that autumn I was sick constantly. It was after a month of illness that I figured out what I'd done and changed the scenario. I got better within a week. On one hand we had more staff sick days after that, but on the other hand I didn't die!

When you look at a psychic or energetic drain, it resembles a tube coming from someone and attaching itself to your body. At the attachment site there may be hooks or some sort of suction feature. Don't be alarmed or frightened. Keep calm and don't react. We will tell you how to deal with drains in short order.

The drain will frequently settle on a chakra or area of your body where your aura is weakest. Weaknesses in the aura can be found where the physical body is weaker, has suffered damage or injury, or where symptoms during illness manifest frequently. If you are able to see or know damage caused in past lives, you could experience weakness in your aura there, too.

These puppies hurt like hell when you first get them, and although you will not be able to ignore them as you might with hooks, long-term drains do become numb.

Clearing a Drain

Taking care of a drain is important, as they can really ruin your day. First thing to do is call upon a lightworker to help you. Give Archangel Michael a call and ask that the drain be removed from you and put in the earth. This way the sender can get all the energy they need free and clear of your stuff. When they get earth energy, it is clearer, lasts longer, and is more healing to them.

If you are dealing with a reverse drain, ask for help with removing the toxins and soul parts too. We call the goddess Kwan Yin to help clear the soul parts and goddess Brigid or the hazmat team to clear the toxins. You will also need the hole in your aura repaired. Archangel Raphael is the one to call for all healing needs.

Don't forget to look for the contract, legacy, belief, fear, etc., that allowed the drain to attach to you in the first place. Ask these questions: Why did I allow this? Do I have a contract or soul part that needs help? A stronger, more self aware you is the best defense against drains.

As we organize all this information in a nice tidy package of self-awareness, remember that the promises you made long ago live in your subconscious and don't reveal themselves until you try to do something radical in your life. It's great to grow up and change; we thoroughly support you in that. So, if you hit resistance to your next move up the enlightenment ladder, don't give up. You've just stepped on a contract, a vow, or a curse. As we've shown, they are easily made and easily broken in the Akashic records.

Please, please, please do your part in preventing forest fires of the soul and deal with your hooks and drains. All those drains contribute to escalated crabbiness and can cause wars. Give peace a chance and dump your hooks and drains.

Chapter 12

Battle Cry "Hell No, We Won't Go!"— Your Fears, Beliefs, Stains, and Blocks

Underneath all the layers of contracts, soul parts, and entities, you will find fear at the base of it all. Before we say
one more word about fear, let us share encouragement and a spot
of wisdom from Eleanor Roosevelt: "You gain strength, courage,
and confidence by every experience in which you really stop and
look fear in the face. You must do the things which you think you
cannot do."

Now, back to your regularly scheduled lecture. Your fears are
first in line with the biggest voices, and they will tell you that
you can't do anything—or, more specifically, that thing. Fears are
the root causes of your blind spots, and they stop you in your
tracks with convincing evidence that there are no solutions or
choices. And if that doesn't work, they trigger hormonal chaos
that confuses your brain and has you braced for fight or flight.
It's like your fears are sentient beings that exist solely to plot your
demise. Well, in a way they are, because they are a part of your
consciousness, and you really can't escape yourself; you can only
deny yourself.

When you are stuck, regressing, in pain, confused, or just generally in a bad space, it is because you handed the keys to the
Cadillac to your fears and they've taken the exit to the bad part
of town. Suddenly you're in a B-grade horror movie, and you're
sure you're one of the minor characters who ends up with an axe

in your head. Wow, palms are getting sweaty already just reading this! Fears are just that wily, and they can cue up that film, direct blame, and justify chickening out in 2.2 seconds.

Fears also have a seductive side to them. They say, "*Nooooo, we're not the problem—it's them, it's the government, it's the man.*" They say this to you in a sultry, deep voice that you can't resist, and then you decide to blame dumb luck or the rest of the world for the phobias you keep. Tricky little bastards, aren't they? Your fears and blocks won't let you win—they make you believe your own negative press.

It is amazing how a fear created by a traumatic event will go out and replicate itself by exposing you to drama that proves its self-fulfilling prophecy. The fear basically takes the light you bring into your life and feeds off of it and uses dirty pool to get its own way. Your fear can and will travel lifetime to lifetime until it's dissolved. Just thought you might like to know that.

Every type of Akashic healing you experience will contain a fear, a block, a belief, and a stain. The difference between a fear, a belief, a stain, and a block is in how they are all layered upon each other. One begets the others, and at the root of it all is fear.

Fear

It all starts with the fear that is born out of a difficult emotional experience. That experience was more painful than you ever wanted to handle and certainly never want to again. Your fear lives off that vow of "never again" and morphs into many incarnations to keep you to your promise.

Belief

When the fear has moved in, gotten comfortable, and put its feet up on your coffee table, it has graduated into a belief. A belief that if you ever did that thing again it would be worse than before and you definitely will not survive it. A belief like this is the next step in your shutting down.

Stain

As this fear-turned-belief gains strength in your life, it becomes a stain that you see life through. A stain is a distortion of perception or filter on your ability to experience truth. It colors the way you expect life to be, where even happy events are colored with your underlying belief and fear. This is where you've become frozen in fear and you've determined that it is no longer safe to (fill in the blank).

Block

When it all comes together, the fear, belief, and stain, you now have a full-fledged block. This block becomes a tangible reality because you have embraced this fear as a reality and truth. It is your perfect blind spot that says: "Do not enter," "these are not the droids you are looking for," "ignore the man behind the curtain," "there is no problem here," "hell no, we won't go," or "I have no choice!" When you push up against this block by changing your behavior, taking a risk, or starting the healing process, it can actually make you sick. If you are to just white-knuckle it and do what good ole Eleanor Roosevelt said and look fear in the face, it could all end in tears and soiled pants. But we'll have none of that! We say do the work beforehand and clear that bugger out of your story first, and then follow dear Eleanor's advice.

How many people have you met or heard about whose lives fall apart once they've achieved their dreams? We have all seen this scenario in action, and Alanis Morissette even wrote a song about it, "Ironic." Isn't it ironic? Your fears in action are the reason that there is no magic pill or vision board that will work, because the minute you get some traction that little so-and-so will show you who is really boss in your waking life by sabotaging your every move. Don't be a hater now, it's doing this to protect you. You have unresolved trauma, and the fear has been created to support you in that reality. What needs to happen here is a personal shift by resolving the trauma. Then fear will dissolve.

Armed with this awareness, you can now go into your Akashic records and show that underlying fear who is boss. Who's the boss, you ask? Well it's you and your relationship to the Divine, of course! When you address your fears in the Akasha, you have a support staff of experts who will face that fear with you and help you clear it. How perfect is that; your fear makes you feel alone, yet when you look at it in your records, you immediately prove it wrong! Brilliant, and on the right side of ironic.

We broke the cycle of fear into these four layers for you because that is how you will find them. The reason or root cause of your fear hides beneath them, and now that you know the code of what to look for you are locked and loaded for some fear hunting.

Akashic Tales from Aunt Jacki

For ten years I refused to see a dentist because I was terrified of them. At the ten-year mark I could honestly call this fear a block. Finally, my loving sister made us both appointments, and I white-knuckled my way through. Before the hygienist could finish cleaning my teeth, though, I had to leave because the dentist started lecturing me.

It took another four years for me to seek out a dentist, and I did it only because I had to take my daughter. I sat in the dentist chair after getting the X-rays and video taken of my teeth. They left the images up on the monitor, and I had a panic attack and had to reschedule my cleaning. This was ridiculous; I had to address this dental fear.

I knew why I was afraid. When I was a child, my dentist didn't believe in using Novocain for little cavities or less than two fillings (it slowed him down). I am one of nine children, and I listened to my siblings scream as they got their fillings done; then it was my turn at the end.

Holy crap! I couldn't clear this one on my own. I needed help, and the talented Patty Shaw was on hand for this nightmare (in the past and currently). We took the adrenalin out of the trauma so I could clear the belief and stain, and thus dismantle the block.

I am happy to report that my last two dentists have been wonderful, and one was even a bit flirty. The only thing that scares me about dentists now is the bill.

In your waking life you will find that there are things you just won't do, and no one can make you. Or there is a behavior that doesn't make sense, but you do it anyway or unconsciously. When you come across those triggers in your life, it's time to step into your records and take charge in that dimension so you can take charge in your waking life.

What does all this look like in the Akashic records? Perfectly reasonable question, and we'll endeavor to describe how these elements have been presented to us. Of course, we have to repeat that you and your guides will have your own special relationship and language, but here's a jumping-off point to get you started.

Fear: White Knuckles and Silent Screams

Just try and look at a fear square on and you will constantly see the last little bit of it slipping out of your line of vision. They are quick, slippery, and savvy shape-shifters, and they'll always leave you with a cold shiver going up your spine and secretly glad you just missed them. What did you expect from fear, anyway? Your fears will almost always look and feel like dangerous monsters waiting in the shadows with untold terrors that'll make you pee your pants, but once you put the light of the Divine on them, you will discover that they are just little worms that cast big shadows. It's your expectation that you'll fail that keeps fear large and looming, and the only way to cure that is to hunt it down and deal with it.

Don't be afraid, it's only your Akashic records. Actually, go ahead and be afraid. But bring a bucket of courage with you and a flashlight. It seems like when you start to deal with fears, it can get a little dark. Makes sense, since monsters only live in the dark so we can clearly see their glowing eyes (it's all for effect).

As you hunt around your Akashic record room looking for the thing that defines your fear, move slowly and let it come to you. One strategy you can use is to set a trap and use yourself as the bait. Frankly, fear is quite egotistical; it struts its stuff all over your convictions and courage, and that is exactly how you'll get your fear's attention and lure it into your trap. Even if you have to fake it, muster up some courage and tell fear your plans. The rest, they say, is history (or herstory) of how you and your spiritual bouncers cornered the source of your fears and phobias, took control, and watched them fade into the sunset.

Believe It or Not!

Your beliefs are the materials you build your life with. Without them you would not have the foundation, walls, and ceilings to your Akashic record room. It's what we believe in that makes up our reality. Even though our beliefs can cause trouble in our life, they are really quite neutral. They are just what we call our truth in the moment.

We know what our life looks like, but what does a belief look like? Does it have substance, or is it a wispy thing that floats around? Truth be told, we see signs, ticker tape, and sticky notes that literally tell us the current beliefs we are operating under. Occasionally a guide will show up with a scroll to emphasize the age of the belief (the older the belief is, the older the message delivery system). Do not be offended by cave drawings; they are not telling you that you need pictures in order to understand the concept. They are telling you this is old stuff, man. Sometimes it's hard to read the words in the records. This may be part of the block or resistance, or it could be because the lighting is too low. No matter what the reason is, you can always ask a guide to help you out. They may even read it to you.

Beliefs are born of fears, but sometimes those fears and beliefs are inherited through family, culture, community, and general mass hysteria. Advertising is another way to seed your fears into beliefs, with those beliefs becoming the benchmark through which you make your decisions. Before you jump on the haters or scaredy-cat bandwagon, take a peek in your records to see if you grabbed on to someone else's fear and made it your very own.

Stains: *Oooo,* Shiny

Is looking at life through rose-colored glasses a blessing? If they keep you from truth and personal empowerment, we think you ought to trade them in for something less Pollyanna. Upon your next trip to your records if you see blotches of color on the walls, ceiling, or floor, you are being shown that you've got some perception problems. These pieces of colored plate glass randomly placed about the place are stains. They can be any size, color, and density, but they are always see-through, if only somewhat. They distort your vision, and each one acts as a filter through which you view the world and the world is reflected back to you.

Stains can really do a number on how you interpret people's words and actions, and you can often sabotage yourself based on the theme of these stains. For example, there can be a stain that keeps you feeling taken advantage of, and another stain that makes you feel like life is a burden and you don't have any good luck. Both stains zap your joy and optimism and get in the way of your success.

Stains can also run in the family as well as be a personal stain. It can even be a stain that affects the entire culture you were born into. All are cleared the same way.

Once you examine a stain or two, you may pick up on a pattern. Multiple stains are usually variations on a theme, and they'll all show up together, which makes clearing them easy and efficient. Many of your stains are revealed through the negative self-talk you can't seem to shut out of your head. You will also see the effect of a stain in your behaviors and the way you make decisions. If you keep expecting to hear, "Wow she's such a (fill in the blank with your favorite insult)," you have got yourself a stain. Tsk-tsk.

✒ Stain Chatter in the Akashic Records with Patty

I've had a hell of a time jump-starting my confidence as a healer and teacher, and it was really becoming a liability for me. For a very long time, I subscribed to the Eleanor Roosevelt school of looking fear in the face and doing it anyway. I rebelled against my fear and tried to exorcise it out of my life by sheer will power and orneriness. What I got was an ulcer, and a weird hiving pattern on my neck and chest that always gave me away. (Just put a "kick me" sign on my back and call it a day, will ya!)

When I started clearing the stains I found in my records that screamed "I'm too flawed" and "I need to keep my mouth shut and stay out of the limelight," my efforts to become a better public speaker, handle conflict, and be a friend were smoother and more natural. I started to notice confidence within myself. I really love this tool and am thrilled the guides showed it to us.

Blocks Are for Blockheads

Your block is the belief, stain, or fear in action. It stops you from moving forward or sabotages your intent, sometimes before it even has a chance to begin. A block holds one or all of the elements of your fear, belief, or stain.

Lucy called Charlie Brown a blockhead because he kept letting her hold the football while he wound up for the greatest kick of his life. He did this over and over, even though they both knew she was going to pull the ball away at the last second. He refused to learn, and she took full advantage of that. Blocks are just like that. They keep you from seeing that you're stuck and repeating the same action in spite of how the situation looks to you. Sorry, but you're being a blockhead. In your records, blocks will look just like they sound: a block of energy (although we have seen blocks that look like linebackers, sumo wrestlers, and police barricades). The energy feels dense and impenetrable by any force. It's not, but it feels that way. Hard as you try, you won't see your way into, through, or around a block without the help of your guides and some well-placed questions. They are literally a blind spot in your psyche hiding the answer of how to do things differently.

Two Ways to Address Healing Your Fears

It's your big moment. You know what issue you're going to tackle, and you get stopped by white noise and a churning gut. This is your signal that your ego has put the brakes on and you've walked right smack into something substantial—the block. This is actually a good thing, so take a deep breath and call on the team. You're going in.

When we give you the evolution/de-evolution choice, we mean you can open this can of worms from the top or the bottom. The goal here is to just get in and start undoing the pattern and getting yourself free of its spell. If you start in the middle it's OK too, but you may want to keep a notebook by your side to keep score and make sure you got all the pieces and parts.

Taking the Evolution of a Fear Path

If you find the fear first, you'll know because you'll feel it in your body. It feels nasty, creepy, and you won't want to look at it. Also you won't want to believe that this is true about you because you have been fighting this feeling all along. What you do first is call upon your warrior, guide, or angel to come and take possession of it. They'll grab a hold of it and put it up to the litmus test of the light or truth.

We love to call upon Archangel Khamael for this because he's already mastered fear and knows how to deal with it in a discerning way. This archangel is more than your garden variety brave heart; he understands that people tend to overblow their perception of the power fear really has. He also likes to hold up your fears by the scruff of their neck and let them struggle a bit. That takes some of the wind out of the fear!

Step 1: Suss Out Fear

Once your fear is in custody, give it its day in court and listen to what it's saying. Giving it its voice will bring out much more than what you're scared of. This will be very illuminating.

✐ True Confessions

We both have a fear of not being good enough. It's a rare person who escapes this fear, but here we are writing this book together, sobbing about our inferiority complexes. If we can face our fears, so can you.

One thing that is wrapped up in your fear is your ego. Fear is the alarm to a threat, and its ego's job to respond to that threat, *tout de suite*. Your ego could respond in many different ways; find out what yours is doing. Is it puffing you up and making you defensive, or are you going to play victim and see how that works for you? This information will be important as you move ahead to learn about your beliefs around you and the situation.

🖋 True Confessions

Our ego response to our fear has been to overcompensate for our perceived inadequacies, which triggered variations of jealousy, envy, and self-doubt. Basically, our egos were all over the "who's writing better than whom?" map. Sheesh.

Find out how long you have had this fear. Is it something you started earlier in your life, or did you bring it from another life experience? Is this something from a recent experience? If so, you will want to get on that before it digs its talons in. Knowing this will change the parameters of your search.

🖋 True Confessions

We found out that our souls have been overcoming self-worth fears for lifetimes. This means this is really a lesson or a mission to master our lesson.

Ask your guides to show you what original experience gave birth to this fear. Here you'll have to suspend your judgment because they may tell you something you can't quite wrap your head around. It's OK, just go with it. Ego test: if the answer is really general or grandiose, you are still focused on the fear and your ego. The answer needs to be very personal.

🖋 True Confessions

For us the original experience was making a big spiritual mistake and not being able to forgive ourselves.

Release the fear and invite in the gift. Ask Archangel Khamael to remove the fear from you, now that you know the story and are ready to let it go. Feel that fear being released and then look for the void that was left by it. You always have to fill that void. Oddly, when you let something go, you don't automatically fill that space with yourself, like water and air do. You have to invite something in. Your gift can be your own divine self or it can be something that represents overcoming this fear and giving you strength and courage. Bring this energy right into your body, too.

Step 2: Test Your Beliefs

Now that you have neutered your fear-ego response, go get that next incarnation of your fear: the belief. The key to working with a belief is that it involves your thoughts. It is something you decided about yourself to make the fear manageable. Often your ego plays a hand in the creation of your belief; it gives you the idea that you are a certain way so it can control your moves.

Unless you inherited this belief from family or your larger community, this belief is also very personal and speaks of your own behavior. Dealing with a family belief or social belief will have its personal component, but you'll have to do the translating for yourself. It's not too hard, it's just a matter of being really honest and observant.

Your next step is to decide if this belief is still in good form or if it's part of the problem. Let's say it's part of the problem. Then you'll want to make some changes. It's definitely time for a rewrite. We love rewrites because you can take your time and try on a few different scripts and you get to see the record keepers in action. Patty always pictures a quill writing of its own accord on a piece of parchment. Very Hogwarts.

By all means, call upon your guides to help you do the rewrite. They've got your back on this and will always help you rise to the next best version of yourself with each edition. Archangel Gabriel is perfect for this job, as is the goddess Brigid.

Some things to consider for the rewrite:

* Make the words transformational—i.e., go from a limiting behavior to a freer one. For example, say you have a belief that states, "I have the worst luck. Anything that can go wrong will go wrong." Rewrite that belief to a freer way of experiencing life: "As I am presented with challenges, I have the wisdom, tenacity, and attitude to resolve and overcome them in a positive way,"

* Keep it positive and realistic—no need for overachieving or narcissistic tendencies here.

* Listen for more ego responses and counter them in the rewrite—e.g., "It won't stick," "You'll fail tomorrow."

* Make the rewritten belief a gift to yourself—it is going to replace the energy that was there before, so make it something you will love to live with. Give it the woo-hoo factor.

While you are doing all of this evaluating and rewriting, you may feel it in your body. Sometimes change hurts. This is because all the toxic energy, wounded soul parts, and entities that are wrapped up in this process are getting shaken up and trying to bubble to the surface. If this is what's going on for you, call upon a healer-guide (Archangel Raphael), or even your warrior (Archangel Khamael) to soothe you and hold you steady while you finish your work. Now go edit and make it awesome.

Step 3: Out, Damned Spot!

Take a look around your room. You got a stain? No problem, we have a process for that, too. What you've been afraid of all this time has morphed into a filter and is clouding your judgment. Stains are pretty easy to clear up. Many times they clear up automatically as you face your fear and rewrite your belief. Others need you to deconstruct the block before they can completely dissolve. Very much like the other manifestations of your fear, you can release the stain by naming its distortion and choosing to let it go. Our favorite archangel for dissolving stains is Gabriel. She's excellent in destroying the lies and fears you're using to color your world.

✒ True Confessions

We both had the stain that kept us seeing the other as a specific personality type and behavior. We used this distortion to anticipate each other. Jacki was to always be the extrovert and Patty the introvert, and that was that. Imagine the confusion and reactions when roles suddenly were reversed or merged. Oy!

Step 4: Stop Being Such a Square

The *pièce de résistance* to this whole exercise is the block. Once you work this puppy out, it all finally comes together and makes sense. If you look at the block as the box that contains the fear, stain, and belief, you will understand why we suggest you deal with all these elements before you walk away. Your healing will be just that much more complete.

The final manifestation of this particular fear is the big bad block that takes up space in your Akashic record room and your life and a total game-changer. Hang in there, you are almost done! Identifying the block is all about tricking it into revealing its purpose. It's not going to come right out and tell you because it's a block. It will cause you to think you've become blind, deaf, and dumb first, but don't panic; call in the helpers.

✒ True Confessions

When Jacki was looking for her block about writing, it literally was a blank wall and she thought nothing was there. Patty saw a dark field of nothing, making it seem like she was lost.

Here are the last steps you'll need to do to unlock the block box and evolve that fear right out of your life.

First, look for the "tell." This is something that demonstrates the reason for the block. Look on all sides or use your X-ray vision to peer inside for clues. It could be a statement, a feeling, or a knowing. If you see nothing, that could be a clue, too. Step back and reflect on what the "nothing" means to you and what you are afraid of. Many times a block grows out of your emotional outcry that this is the last straw. An energetic fortress begins to erect itself around the fear. This is what you are working on taking down.

Next, make your choice to not be blocked in this way. Call in the team to help you flush out the meaning of the block. You may have to pull a Luke Skywalker and stop looking at the block to see and understand it. Use the rest of your "knowing" senses to unravel the story.

To release the block, call upon a divine being to detox you and your Akashic room. (See chapter 8 for a list of contenders.) You may experience the block just disintegrating since you have cleared what was filling it, so you may need extra assistance. Buddha is an excellent guide for mastering letting go. He helps you see what limitations you are creating by hanging on to the block. Archangel Haniel brings victory when you use joy and love. She will show you how to release the block and refill with divine love. If the block is particularly stubborn, the goddess Kali will kick it down for you. If you end up calling Kali for assistance, make sure to look for other soul parts connected to that block that may have been holding it in place.

Finally, in this last step you will fill yourself with a gift. This can be your own divinity or a symbol that represents you without the block. Gifts are typically the inverse of the fear, but we don't mean its exact opposite. The gift is something that heals the reason the block was created. Archangel Haniel is a loving guide who can help you find your gift if you are having trouble seeing it.

> ## 🖋 A True Confession and a Happy Ending
>
> Our gift to us as we released and healed our block was peace.
> We are enough as we are and are already filled with the light.

De-evolution of a Block: Starting with the Block and Working Toward the Fear

We can't tell you how many times we or our clients couldn't contemplate what the fear might be that is affecting their life. All we know is that life isn't working the way we want it to. We keep hitting the same wall or limitation, and the results don't change no matter what type of external adjustment we are making. You know that definition of insanity that everyone is talking about, the one where you are so invested in your own fears and beliefs that you can't see the block they created or even contemplate that this may be bad for you?

When you are that kind of stuck, you start with the wall you are bumping up against. Here's a clue—that wall *is* your block, and you start the process by unraveling it first to take a peek under the hood. When taking the bottom-up approach, you start with your block, then move your way up through the layers to the fear. We call this de-evolving the block!

Step 1: Open Up Pandora's Box

Instead of releasing evil unto the world, you are taking authority over your block and putting yourself back in the driver's seat. Start by naming the block as you see it in this moment. An example from Jacki, "I stare and stare at my computer, but my mind won't rest on what I need to do so I keep opening up Facebook." or "I joined Weight Watchers, went to my first meeting, and then went out to dinner with my friends where I totally forgot my plan and ordered lobster mac and cheese." Here's a few good ones from our clients: "I don't have enough money for rent again." Or how about,

"I did it again; I let them walk all over me and didn't speak my mind." And don't forget the elusive "I don't know what I want and can't make up my mind."

Looking at and naming these blocks open you up for the whole story from your Akashic record guides and helps you see what energetic form this block has taken in your records.

✒ Akashic Tales from Aunt Jacki

When I was working on one of the many issues I have with money, I couldn't even see the block until I started naming how it manifested in my life with frequently being short of cash at the last minute. Initially I saw a giant hole with nothing in it. I continued to talk about what was happening over and over again and asked to see what this block really was. My divine allies showed me the block as a money leak in my checkbook. That was the opposite of what I was expecting. So, I set aside some time to look at my expenses. I analyzed what I was spending my money on and how often I was balancing my checkbook, and why I felt I couldn't keep money. This led me to a belief that being spiritual and monetarily wealthy were mutually exclusive ideas, and I immediately made that a healing priority!

Step 2: Take Off the Rose-Colored Glasses

Now that you see the block you can pop the hood and ask to see what this block is made of. Initially you will see the filter that you are looking through at life. This is the first illusion that you cast upon yourself. The stain will force you to view your situation in terms like: everything, always, and never. Your logic knows that can't be true, nothing is that consistent; but your logic is not in charge here, your fear is. When you name that stain, call it out into the light, you can see it for what it is and look past it into the truth.

Your stain is very immature; kids look at life through the colored glasses of the moment. They will complain that you *never* do anything fun when they don't want to do their chores. The stain gives you permission to be passive, and even a victim to circumstances—or worse. Stains take away your options and validate the reactions the fears perpetuate.

Ask Archangel Haniel to take authority over the stain and let you see what is beyond it without its distortion. You will then be looking into the face of your belief in action. As you let the story continue to unfold, make sure you take copious notes. You will need them before this journey is over.

Step 3: Can You or Can't You?—Your Belief Tells the Tale

The block is opened, the stain is lifted, and now you can see the fearful conclusion that is defining everything for you. The belief that is running off of this fear that you have yet to name created the stain you were looking through. It is easy to see now that the stain is out of the way, and it is now time to name that belief. Write it down, say it out loud, and really understand it. It feels so powerful and true, doesn't it? Yet it no longer rings true, because something is wrong with it and it no longer resonates with you.

Ask your divine guides to illuminate this belief within the light of the creator. What you will see immediately is what idea your fear overlaid upon a healthy belief. You will see the illusion and then the truth beneath it. Beliefs are what keep us going day to day, and there is always something positive within them that helped you survive a stressful situation.

When you pull off the illusion and leave the truth, you will be able to identify the fear that started this whole mess. Ask your guides to hang on to that illusion for you as you finish this process. Look at the healthy belief that was under the illusion and see if it needs a bit of tweaking and rewriting. If you have been calling to the archangels, you probably have Khamael, Gabriel, and Haniel in the room already. Khamael can hang on to the illusion while Gabriel and Haniel help you do a bit of creative and joyful rewriting.

Step 4: Those Fears Are Dead to Me!

Nothing but the fear is left now, and it is pissed! You've removed all of its backup systems (although it may be hiding a few more), but it is naked in front of you and it will work hard to deflect you from it. You may get crazy, woo-woo–making stories about Atlantis and aliens, or it will be so far removed from what your initial block is that it doesn't seem real. That is because it is throwing you a red herring over and over again to distract you and save itself.

Your ego is helping it, too. Your ego uses your fear as a defense mechanism to save it from pain, so you have to get trickier than the fear by going around it. If your fear is still in hiding, ask your ego what it needs to be able to move forward without the fear. Ha! Take that, you silly fear!

Your fear is outed now, either by you being able to see it for what it is, or you tricking it by seeing what you need to counter it. Talk this fear out, verbally and on paper. You are in the home stretch, and you need to put it all together soon and release the whole thing. Archangel Khamael will take authority over your fear, holding it away from you so you can see it in the light and for what it really is. It's in the spotlight, and now you can interrogate it to find what the truth is under all its illusions.

Step 5: Age Before Beauty, Pearls Before Swine— How Old Is This Fear?

Is this fear from a past life, childhood, or the present? You will find layered experiences that prove this fear, so as you find them, keep asking to be taken back to the oldest one. Keep going until you feel the ring of truth, until your guides confirm that, yup, that's it! Go to that moment and ask to see the experience that created the fear and all the players in it. Ask to see the fears of the other people involved, their agendas, and what the universal truth of the situation is. That changes the game right there. You can bring in the understanding of how the others in the situation were working, not from truth, but from fear. You can see how your trauma of the moment created this fear, and then you can ask it to be released back into the earth to be recycled or burned up in the cauldron.

This whole picture—the fear and its origin, the belief, the stain, and the block that came from them all—should make sense now. You can see a complete story, and you can let it go now. Your guides help lift it and all related energy away from you. You are now ready for your prize!

Step 6: Give Yourself a Gift

When you clear that big mess, there is always a hole to fill in. If you don't fill it with light and love, it will fill in with other fears or new fears. You will feel within your body where that void is; something will feel uncomfortable, weak, cold, or buzzy, and that is where you bring your focus. Ask Metatron to bring a new truth to you to manifest and replace the old belief and fear. Let that light mix with your energy and fill in this void. As it fills in, you will find a gift to help you manifest your new belief. Cherish that gift by writing down what it is and how you will use it to better yourself.

Everything's Coming Up Roses

Congratulations, you did it! Now go live it! Fears are at the heart of so much of your troubles, and so many other issues are triggered by them. Celebrate when you find another challenge is shaken loose by the work you did; it's another step in your personal evolution and one step closer to the Divine and having the life you truly desire. Start this new, fear-free reality by creating new and healthy spiritual habits to replace the ones you just cleared.

Chapter 13

The Akashic Wisdom Process, a.k.a. the Rhythm Method

Life is messy, and so are your Akashic records. Sometimes they will be a consummate representation of your chaos; other times they will be the proverbial light at the end of the tunnel. While exploring your records you will inevitably be reminded of your imperfections and the pain you've suffered at the hands of another, and possibly yourself. When these issues are cause for concern, it's time to step into your records and see why bad things happen to good people. Just remember, you will not find anything in your records that cannot be healed, fixed, saved, helped, or cleared, and your Akashic pals are waiting and will help you find all the stuff you are ready to graduate past!

Throughout this book we've presented all the pieces and parts of the Akashic records that we know of, and we want to make sure you understand that they are all connected in some fashion or another. When taken together, these pieces help you understand your story and ultimately move past the ways it limits you. So, when you step into your records for a self-healing session and find there are lots of spiritual issues to wade through, be confident that there is always a workable way to address each and every one.

Not sure what to start with? Are your questions answered by a deafening silence? We have a process for that. Please let us present our Akashic Wisdom Process, or the Rhythm Method. Try it out and remember to begin your journey with answering the question about what's going on today.

Begin with What Is Bothering You Most

The "scratch to our itch" lives in the center of our inner ball of twine, and the first thing you need to do is find the end and start working it loose. Then, let the ball unravel to reveal everything that contributes to said itch. When you get to the other end, you'll find that there is no ball and there is no more itch. Whether you like layers or balls of twine, your healing path will be revealed to you one experience at a time until you get to the very first event: the core. Once the core issue is resolved, you will be the master of that subject once and for all.

The biggest clue as to where to start in your Akashic records is to start with what's bugging you on the surface, right now. Let the issues of your day-to-day life lead you to the beginning of your journey. There is a reason why a particular issue has suddenly become an irritant. It's because you have grown spiritually and emotionally to a place where this fear, block, or issue in general no longer makes sense. You have learned everything you can from this subject and are ready to get rid of the junk that's left over (kind of like a spiritual digestive system). Don't panic, this is just your higher self telling you what's up next from your Akashic job jar. Take your time, be thorough, and don't give up. You will get there.

The beautiful thing about the Akashic realm is that there are no limits to what you can use it for. As healers, though, we tend to gravitate toward making changes that will make life easier and more joyful. Yes, yes, we know there is karma and that challenge spurns creativity, but there is no hard-and-fast rule saying you have to be miserable the entire time. In fact, inspired creativity is joyous, and karma doesn't have to be a bitch to be balanced.

This step-by-step Akashic Wisdom Process can be used with any issue you have and can be tailored to your unique situation. Enjoy the journey; it's more freeing than you know. *Psst*—please take notes! You never know, it may become a best seller.

The Process

The Akashic Wisdom Process will take you on a journey to find all of your broken pieces and understand the story they tell you about why you are here and what isn't working in your life. Once you know your story, you can identify how it is affecting your waking life. These reactions manifest as the fears, blocks, contracts, and soul parts in your Akashic records.

As you visit your records more and more, you will begin to notice a rhythm to your healing, too. Just as stories have a beginning, a middle, and an end, your answers will also be presented in a rhythmic pattern. Our job is to help you establish your rhythm and ride it out to the end. When you are done with this process, you will remember how good life can be and be energized to share it with others! Ready, set, let's get started on the Akashic Wisdom Process!

Finding What's Blocking Your Success

Step 1: Find the Story Behind the Issue

This story is the evidence of what you manifested in your life based on your experiences. Allow as many details as possible to come to the surface by letting the plot thicken and the characters develop. Then you will really begin to see why your life is the way it is. You can do this by following your broken bits back to their beginning. Let the story play out to the end; don't be in a rush or you will miss something.

Your story may have many chapters, which means it could cover many decades of your life. Remember that you are painting the picture around why you are struggling today. To stay focused on the issue you are working with, keep reminding yourself that you are looking for everything that contributed to the reason you are here in your Akashic records, including everything that is ready to release. Ask yourself, "What happened in my past that has made me have this dysfunction in my current life?"

You may find yourself feeling your story in your body. If you do, talk to that indigestion or headache or heartache and let it be another hint. Indigestion can be a side effect of fear; a headache can be caused by stress or conflicting thoughts you're trying to reconcile. The ache in your heart could be about a loss, a lack of forgiveness, or guilt or shame you are holding on to. To help you tell the story as fully as possible, here are some questions for you to answer. If the pain gets to be too much, ask the Akashic record keepers to hold this pain away from you while you unravel the big picture.

We're going to demonstrate this process with our example client, who we always call Betty. Betty came to us frustrated with her life. She felt ineffectual, passed over, and unfulfilled. We put some of her answers to the questions below to help you with your own answers.

Ask these questions of yourself to get started in uncovering your story:

* **Q: What has happened in my past that has made me have this dysfunction in my life?**

* A: I was ignored by my parents, my husband neglects me, and I can't seem to get any traction at my job. I haven't had a raise in three years.

* **Q: Where does the story begin?**

* A: It all began with my childhood.

* **Q: Who is in the story?**

* A: My parents and I.

* **Q: Is there a backstory? What is it?**

* A: My parents both are quiet people and keep to themselves. My grandparents on both sides were hard workers, but they never seemed to make much money. I think they were basically happy, though.

* **Q: What emotions come up while telling the story?**

* A: Anger, frustration, sadness, fear? I feel sad and rejected. Unloved.

* **Q: What do you regret? What have you done wrong?**

* A: I regret feeling unwanted and not knowing what to do about it. I wish I could see my parents in another way. I really don't know what I did wrong.

* **Q: What is the underlying theme of all the events of the story?**

* A: I was so hurt by being ignored as a child that I decided to not bother anyone with my needs and started taking care of myself. I decided to never expect anyone to need me or want to help me. Today I am in a dead-end job, my husband is too busy to take a vacation with the family, and I find I am doing so much for my children they don't know how to even pour a bowl of cereal for themselves.

Step 2: Note Your Reaction to Your Story

You see the reaction to your story in the beliefs, thought forms, fears, and contracts you create around yourself and the other people in your story. These are also the building blocks of your world, the waking world you live in every day. Our example client Betty said, "I felt my parents were dismissive of me and they didn't listen to what I said. I actually believed that I was insignificant and didn't have anything worthwhile to contribute." What Betty created in her world to support her belief was being passed over for raises and promotions, being ignored by her spouse, and being taken advantage of in many ways.

Following are some questions to help you find your reactions and see how you've converted them into various vows, contracts, or beliefs. Don't worry about dealing with these beliefs yet—that will come down the line, in step 7. Right now you are just pinpointing issues and taking note.

* **Q: What has this issue cost you in your life?**

* A: Intimacy, respect, happiness.

* **Q: What is preventing you from reaching your goal?**

* A: Not asking for a raise, resenting my spouse instead of talking to him, being a slave to our children. That all has stopped me from feeling loved and appreciated.

* **Q: What did you do to handle the pain?**

* A: I struggled to get positive attention from my parents, so I made a personal choice or promise to always be a good child. No matter what was going on or what sacrifices I needed to make.

* **Q: How old were you when you made your vow or promise?**

* A: I was a young child.

* **Q: What do you hear when you ask yourself to go for each of the things you want?**

* A: I can't believe that I'll be given that, and I don't deserve it anyway.

* **Q: Look around your Akashic records; do you see evidence of a contract with anyone in your life to support your beliefs? What does it say, and with whom are you contracted?**

* A: The contract says, "If you take care of me, I'll always love you no matter how much you ignore me." I realize now, I keep remaking this contract with every important relationship.

* **Q: How did the promises and beliefs help you create this block?** (This one is not as easy to answer, so invite your guides to help you. Don't underestimate the power of a simple answer, either.)

* A: After a while I expected to be ignored and forgotten.

* **Q: What are you getting out of staying in your fear?**

* A: I guess my reward is that I don't have to answer to anybody. I can do as I please. Not being accountable is lonely, but it's kinda safe, too. I guess I'm afraid of not being in control.

Step 3: Uncover the Lost Potentials

What shame do you carry around with you because you have manifested issues and short circuits from your story? Let's look at shame in a new light, as a lost potential that connects you to the Divine. This is what you feel ashamed about; not your actions, but the Divine Light you have denied yourself. Shame or lost potential is the opening that your inner saboteur can use to take control of your self-esteem and start driving the bus. That inner saboteur will continually point out how you will never measure up spiritually or otherwise and will keep you focused on the shame and lost potential. Our example client, Betty, manifested her shame or lost potential through the belief that God found her insignificant, and that shame kept her from trying harder, taking risks, and loving herself.

The big G, also known as the Divine Light, the One, Great Spirit, etc., has been a witness to your entire existence. The light knows when is has been denied by you and never holds a grudge. It bears witness to your struggles and loves you even more for them. Shame is when you realize what you've missed out on, and it opens you up to surrendering the pain you have been holding on to. In this stage of your healing you can begin to see who and what needs forgiveness and why.

There is always a gift within your struggle, look for it now. It's OK if you aren't ready to see yet. Let it be and keep going, and through the healing process you will reclaim that potential you thought you lost.

Step 4: Find the Core Thought or Belief to This Issue

In this step, we will trace our story back to the original short circuit or filter responsible for distorting the way you see yourself or your life. This corrupted idea is another way of describing the initial way you broke. The Divine sent you an idea or inspiration, and as it hit your filter, i.e.: your broken piece, it morphed from being something that added to your beauty into something that added to your pain. The vision of your core issue will come to you with the help of your guides.

Be prepared to go deep here, because this core issue may be part of your soul's journey. Relax your expectations and suspend your logic when your guides and divine allies start telling you the story of where it all began. Not every trip into the Akasha rewrites your entire life, but every now and again you catch a wave that takes you to a potential that is beyond your imagination. Crying is OK and expected in the Akasha.

Before you do any exploration, ask Archangel Metatron to take authority over this core issue and all that is involved with it.

* **Q: Ask yourself, What is the fear underneath this block I am dealing with?**

* A: I am not loved or lovable.

* **Q: Ask Metatron, Can you name the truth underneath the issue? (Or, alternatively, ask God, How do you see me?)**

* A: You are priceless and loved deeply by the Divine.

How to Fix It

In these next four steps you will be asked to do many things in order to fix this broken bit that sent you down the rabbit hole. Some of these things will be easy, and others you will balk at. On this part of your journey you will be surrendering all of your broken pieces to the Divine and allowing the Divine to refill you with Truth, the truth it tried to give you originally.

Step 5: Rewriting the Lie

Call upon Archangel Metatron to show you what the Divine's intention is for you. The light or energy that this intention rides on is what will change everything for you and trigger tremendous healing and turn your Titanic around.

* **Q: Ask Metatron if this corrupted idea gets rewritten, or if you will be given a brand-new idea. Is there anything missing?**

* A: My corrupted idea will be rewritten so I am loved. It is up to me to learn how to accept love from others without manipulating.

* **Q: What is your reaction to the new seed? Does your ego react? Name the reactions and know that they are more short circuits or variations of the issue that needs your attention.**

* A: My initial reaction was anger, but then I slowly started feeling ashamed.

* **Q: Do you feel resistance or disbelief that it is possible for things to change?**

* A: I feel hesitant to believe that this can happen for me. I feel isolated—quite empty inside.

* **Q: Do you have any judgments around how things should be?**

* A: I still think my husband should show me more love and affection.

Once you've completed this series of questions, take a moment to surrender your judgments around the Divine's plans for you. This is an exercise in getting out of your own way and accepting the truth. Pay attention to the new or corrected idea you are given. Be clear about what is being healed in you. You will need this information for step 8.

Betty, our example client, was given the gift of self-worth and the wisdom that people need help seeing her worth because of their own blind spots and blocks. She realized that her self-worth is not dependent on how others treat her but is an inherent part of her.

Step 6: Bring the Truth Down into Your Heart

The sixth step is about forgiveness. Surrender your shame and guilt around the way you behaved when your filters and blocks were in action in the past.

Let's talk about this for a moment. You have this short circuit or block you're struggling with, and you put layers and layers of energy (in the form of ideas and decisions) onto it as you keep trying to make sense of what is happening to you. Looking back to the beginning of your issue, you had a choice about what you wanted to do and believe. You could have accepted this truth from the Divine, lived it, and watched where it took you. Or, you could have chosen to change or edit what the Divine gave you to suit your beliefs or manifest your fears. Of course the second choice will cause a distortion of your truth, and the result is missing your mark in life and wondering why things are not going your way. You could even shrug off your responsibilities and blame others for your lot in life.

No matter who helped you get there, be it an entity, a demon, or you own fears, you made a choice to do something different, and it's your God-given right to express your free will. What you are being asked to do here is to be very honest and admit that you made a choice; *you made that choice.* Where the guilt and shame come in is when you try to *not* be responsible for what you chose; when you try to put that responsibility on something outside of yourself. Your efforts to cover this up and try to blame the one who played along in your distortion eventually come back to you as guilt and shame. This is why it's so important to ask for forgiveness, and to extend forgiveness to others.

Forgiveness is not absolution; it is the surrender of the shame that defines your identity or even your relationship to the other party. You don't have to hold on to the pain, remorse, or anger anymore; you are free. Forgiving yourself for feeling shame and guilt lets you see the new potentials you are creating. When you see these new potentials as a truth from the Light, it becomes more real than the lies told by the issues and short circuits that you have been carrying.

Here are some questions you can ask yourself to keep you focused while you work through this process:

* **Q: What would life be like if you surrendered this shame and guilt?**

* A: Life would always be happy, and I would be at peace at work and at home.

* **Q: Now recognize the fantasy that has been running in your Akashic record room. What is the divine truth of your life? What will it look like with these new potentials?**

* A: I see myself making new choices in the moment, asking for help, telling my feelings to others in the moment, and getting listened to.

* **Q: Does this trigger any shame or guilt in you for what has happened in the past?**

* A: It really does. I feel kinda foolish now.

* **Q: What are your feelings of shame or guilt when you think about acting on this new idea?**

* A: I am ashamed that I didn't realize what I was doing all this time. I feel like a dork, like I'm the one who didn't get it.

* **Q: Did you "make a deal with the devil" to keep you safe from your choices in any way?**

* A: I guess so. I wanted to be safe even though I decided to be a wimp.

* **Q: How did any of these choices affect your life?** (This question will spark a review of the issue with the potential of shining a new light of self-responsibility on the situation.)

* A: They really affected my ability to be honest. I wasn't too honest about why I did what I did. Heck, I didn't even know I was playing a game with people. I think this is why I always manipulated people's emotions.

Step 7: Clearing the Contracts and All the Broken Stuff

In this step you will free the destroyed soul parts and soul parts you've collected from others, empower and merge with the ones that want to heal, and dismiss all dark energy in whatever form it takes (inner enemies, entities, or demons). Then you will fill yourself with your light and be healed. Bada boom bada bing! Can we get a hallelujah?

At this point in the process, your experiences, fears, and shortcomings will be validated before you finally release them. The stories you get from this stuff would make the best sci-fi/fantasy book. This is also where you get to discover what makes you tick, and you will get to know your divine allies too. This step takes the most time all of, so go slow, make sure you get everything, take notes, and have fun. Oh, and you get to kick some demon ass. (Who knew you were Buffy in disguise? You were always the chosen one!)

First, list out your short circuits in light of your Truth. Watch as they open up like flowers and reveal their messages.

* **Q: What decisions did you make based on your short circuits? What vows or contracts did you write?**

* A: There was a contract with my husband for him to ignore me so I can feel vindicated in indulging my children. I rewrote these contracts to be more fair, equitable, and loving.

Next, allow all the soul parts that got caught up in these vows and contracts to be revealed. Do you still need to fulfill these vows and contracts? If not, invite in Archangel Michael to cut the ties and Kwan Yin to help heal and place the all soul parts where they belong.

Look around. Do you see any darkness, feel the heebie-jeebies? If in doubt, bring in your Akashic Court (a.k.a. your healing team) along with the record keepers for some serious entity busting. Ask them to take authority over all beliefs, fears, thought forms, and entities of all kinds that are contracted with you in this issue, including demons. Now ask that they be removed from your life and all contracts be voided.

Ask for a thorough detoxing and then slip into the healing waters for a good soak and releasing of pain bodies. The meditation below is for releasing stored up pain from your past. Please enjoy it anytime you feel you need it.

Meditation: Release Your Pain into the Healing Waters

As you prepare for this meditation, become your best friend. You are going to let some old wounds go, and you'll be tempted to do some fancy avoiding or rile yourself up unnecessarily, so you need to be kind and gentle and supportive to yourself.

Next, you'll want to choose the thing you're going to release, so bring to mind an event that represents the pain that you really have not been able to overcome. This is not about reliving it at all. Just be aware of what you want to release. This is about picking the pain du jour and opening the tap. The hardest part about this exercise is being patient while your pain bodies release.

And here we go . . .

Enter your Akashic records the quick and dirty way or the formal way—it's your choice. (You'll find instructions for both in chapter 5.)

Please notice that upon entering your room there is a delightful shallow pool or hot tub for you. It is inviting, and you are drawn to it. This is where you will do the majority of your healing work.

You will need someone to help you release this pain and free you from destructive repeating reactions. This person carries the vibration of a deity, ascended master, or archangel. We're talking top brass here. Any one of these high-level guides is capable of transmuting your pain into love and releasing it into the universe. Pick a guide and invite them into your room and into your healing waters. Can't decide? Select one from our list of guides in chapter 8.

It's time to relinquish your pain body (or bodies) to the universe. Take a deep cleansing breath and let go. It will feel like you've let go of the end of the tightrope, and all your muscles will relax as the stuff at the other end releases. What now begins to move away from you and out of your aura is a shadow of yourself. Many of our clients don't see as much as feel themselves getting lighter, happier, and more relaxed. No matter what you see or don't see, trust that this healing is happening for you. This is like a visit to the spa, so let your guide do the work.

Notice how your guide puts their arms out to embrace your pain body and coax it away from you. Keep letting it go, and if another shadow shows up, let that one slide off as well. Your guide will continue to absorb your pain until you are done. Be relaxed and neutral as this process is happening. Don't concern yourself with the details, as this could cause you to draw the shadow energy back to you.

Now that you have emptied yourself of a significant amount of pain, you need to be filled with something. We suggest you fill yourself with you! Invite the highest, purest version of yourself into all the places where you previously stored your pain body. Take your time and fill every nook and cranny, all the way down to your cells.

Finally, it's time to thank your guide and step out of the pool. Someone is there waiting with a thirsty terry cloth bathrobe. Dry off and notice how awesome you feel! Go ahead, do a happy dance. You've earned it.

Step 8: Anchoring Your New Habits in Your Waking Life

In this final step, you are going to write an action plan that will support you as you embrace your new life. It is based on the story you brought out as you nailed down the root cause of your hang-ups. Your action plan is a list of things you will do differently from now on, and includes what you'll do when you slip up, have doubts, or crumble under the pressure of temptation, momentary weakness, or fear.

1. Make reasonable goals for yourself.

2. As you reach each goal, celebrate yourself and set a new goal.

3. Now describe your new spiritual habit.

4. This new spiritual habit you have created supports the new you. So, write it down and put it on the fridge.

For our example client, Betty, this is what she decided: To communicate more clearly to her husband about her needs and life at home, and to value his process and contribution to the family. To let her children become more independent and responsible for themselves and their actions. To ask for a fair and honest review from her employer, and a plan on how to improve her skills on the job and be rewarded for all she has contributed already. Her new spiritual habit is to remind herself just how valuable she is because she's alive. She'll try not to take the things people do so personally and to do something positively divine for herself every day, even if all she can get in that day is a smile and a wink at herself in the mirror.

Remember, you can recreate your old life and fall back into your old habits and reactions at any time, so be diligent. As you anchor in the new you, ask to be shown what small things in your life trigger you to revert to that old fear and behavior. Your guides will be happy to show you, and you have to be open to believing them. And for goodness' sake, write them down. You won't want to believe what some of your triggers are; you will want to deny that something so silly or simple could throw you off your center, but it can and does if you don't pay attention and let all these things stack up.

Our example client practiced stopping herself from indulging her old habit of assuming her husband was choosing not to be with her whenever he had to work late. Instead, she asked him about his work and drew him in to share with her his dreams and goals for himself. It helped her relate to him as a person and not just her husband and the role he plays in her life.

Next, look for opportunities to anchor in this healing. By this we mean put yourself in situations that let you practice your new spiritual habits. Most of the time they will fall in your lap, but you can create these opportunities as well. Know that when you deal with the people you had contracts with, they may act strange around you. This is an opportunity to behave differently and possibly even explain what your new consciousness is. Or you just say nothing and keep 'em guessing. There is much more power in your actions than your words, and sometimes you need to walk away from relationships that push you back into old, unhealthy, and outdated behavior.

Help others get to your new level by staying in your integrity (and sharing the light). Sharing your light really means reflecting the light to the people around you. What you are doing is saying, "I see the light in you, and I acknowledge it." Period. Validating someone's light is the highest message you can send.

So what does that look like in real life? It means being patient as someone struggles with their own blocks and blind spots. Keep a kind thought for them as their fears do all the talking and possibly attacking. It means getting out of the way and not buying into their illusion. Be in your new integrity, and stay there, and you will be sharing your light.

Here is a list of questions to help you write your action plan:

* What new actions and activities have you added in your life?

* Do you have any reactions to these actions?

* Do you hear any "I can'ts" or "that won't work because"? List them out along with any fears or potential moments of weakness.

* What does your higher self say to your resistance? What does it want you to do when you are flirting with failure, doubt, confusion, or weakness of any kind?

* What is your new way of responding to the same old stresses and conflicts? The answer to this question will help you determine your spiritual habit. It's nice to keep this one in your back pocket for when something comes up suddenly and catches you off guard.

You have just finished the Akashic Wisdom Process and we applaud you. Not because you made it through eight arduous steps, but because you made an important commitment to yourself. It is a very courageous move to look at yourself objectively and honestly. This choice is what it takes to launch your healing journey and each step of the way will bring gifts and freedom.

Chapter 14

Aftercare: Dealing with Akashic Healing Hangovers

You will have a healing crisis after big work in the Akashic records, everyone does, so don't freak out. This happens because your outer world is bouncing off your inner world. The new you is putting out a vibe that contradicts the reality you've already created. It takes time for the two worlds to understand and accept each other. When we say healing crisis, we're talking about the resistance you are experiencing to the new consciousness you've created. You may discover that there is another layer to your issue, and whatever is in it is not only pissed, it is hell-bent on punishing you for daring to clear it out.

This inner battle happens because, for a little while, you are walking in your past and your future at the same time. When you are feeling split, slow down, take some deep breaths, and focus on being in the present. Look at your hands, pay attention to what you are doing right now, and stop thinking about the past or your hopes for the future. Do something mundane, like fold laundry, do the dishes, or your job at work. (I bet your boss will like that answer.)

Many times we have heard from clients about the after-party blues. The reactions can range from flu symptoms to irritation at everyone around you to total meltdown. If you are experiencing a total meltdown, you missed a big piece of puzzle and it's worth your time to go in and find it to heal or blister pack (see page 226) so you can function. The most common reaction to big work, even more common than a healing crisis, is resistance to manifesting the new you in your day to day. You can undo all of the work you just did in your Akashic records, recreate the issue, and then have to clear it again later when you cave to your resistance.

What this looks like basically is, after healing your karmic connection to your ex, you call them and pick a fight about what happened in a past life. Or, worse yet, you chicken out and step right back into the role you are used to playing with them. That is resisting your evolution and sabotaging your efforts. It's OK, you'll get as many chances and opportunities as you need to get it right.

Spiritual Habits (Nuns Have Nuthin' on This)

The most important part of your aftercare is breaking the old spiritual habits and creating new ones. Those old spiritual habits stem from the fear or past life or contract you just worked on. When you step out of the spiritual realm and back into your physical life, it is natural to revert back to your old way of being. We all do it. When life gets kooky and stressful, we go back to the easiest and most successful coping mechanisms from our past—it's human nature, and it's expected. Knowing that this is a likelihood does not doom you to repeating your mistakes, however; let it empower you to purposefully make a new choice. Use your will and desire to guide you.

✒ Akashic Tales from Aunt Jacki

How many times do I need to go into the Akashic records and heal my food issues? How many times do I need to find the past life, mother issue, disconnect from God issue, fear, phobia, etc., that triggers me to overeat and choose the wrong food? I work on it, feel amazing, and still reach for the Captain Crunch the next morning! It's frustrating!

I try and try and try and still go back to the same old habit—until one day when Patty and I went into my records to find the next layer. I was told: "Time to break the habit." I was mad! How dare they say it's now just a habit that I am repeating in my life! How dare those wise beings not understand my compulsion and laziness! It must be some deep past-life trauma from the first century BC that compels me to ignore packing a healthy lunch and then default to eating a Wendy's single with cheese, and of course the accompanying fries and Diet Coke. (For Pete's sake, I got the Diet Coke, didn't I?)

Once I was done with my spiritual temper tantrum, I had to get honest with myself; I have a habit of being lazy and wanting a miracle to help me shed my extra pounds and compel me to be more active in my life. Well shoot! I have had that opportunity with many healings, but my spiritual habit got in the way. If you try to circumvent the process of creating a new habit you will continually fall back to the old one. I am still working on this personally; creating a new spiritual habit, after practicing the old one for forty-four years is going to take a minute to reprogram.

If you just break an old spiritual habit in your Akashic session and don't replace it with a new one, you leave a void. We all know that nature abhors a void and it always fills it with whatever is on hand. In your case, your void will most likely be filled with the spiritual habit you just cleared unless you come prepared. To solidify the healing work you did, fill it with a new spiritual habit and then *do it.* Follow-through is key here. By creating a new habit you are choosing the healing you did on every level.

✒ Aunt Patty's Magic Wands and Wishful Thinking

I sang in the high school choir, and I thought I had a pretty good voice. When Jacki invited me to join the businesswomen of Ferndale in performing solos on stage as a fundraiser, I said, yes, I'd like to do that. Ten minutes later I realized what I had just signed up for and practically made a beeline to a nervous breakdown. I got sick instead.

Over two months of rehearsals and costuming, I ran a fever and was the walking dead. I saw my doctor and my healer. (Yes, I still keep them in separate categories.) While the doc took care of my body, my healer helped me find out why I was reacting so strongly to singing on stage by myself, alone, just me and my piano man, for the first time in my life.

I found loads of reasons for me to have stage fright, and I prayed for a miracle cure for my illness and my fear, but it didn't come. It's not going to come, not in the way I wanted it to. Since the show must go on, I hobbled up on stage when the big day rolled around, dolled up to the nines, and I sang my song. And I survived. Actually, I loved it. My cure will come, but not without practice and letting my inner torch singer out to breathe some fresh air. She's in there, but I abused her so badly that she's hoarse from excessive smoking and hungover. Past lives can be a bitch.

I really wanted to have the magic wand do its magic for me, but that will not make me a singer. Singing will make me a singer. I now take voice lessons and sing badly every week until I can sing well again.

This is where the harder work comes in and you have to consciously repeat the new habit over and over again until you just do it without thinking. In your healing session you got to shortcut a lot of your cause and effect process and you got to find the heart of the matter and heal it; but you cannot completely circumvent the process of learning and evolving. Creating a new habit is the practical application of the healing, and without it you end up with a bit of chaos in your life as you grope for a new way of behaving now that you know better.

One of Jacki's clients was having a major issue around self-acceptance, and it manifested in her belief around beauty. She felt so bad about herself that she did not have a mirror in her house. After a bit of healing work, breaking contracts, and clearing soul parts, it was time to help her create a new spiritual habit. Just because we cleared the messages in her past that said she was ugly and unworthy didn't meant that she would see herself any differently in the mirror. The new spiritual habit was for her to take 365 days of self-portraits with her smartphone. She was to look at these selfies and find one positive thing in the image, then she was to show the images to a trusted loved one and have them tell her what they see in the picture. After one week of doing this, she told Jacki that she could see a change in her face. She was more relaxed in her smile, more open in her face, and she started feeling better about herself. This courageous woman's healing story makes Patty tear up every time she hears it.

Every healing gets a new spiritual habit. Some you are ready for and just need to create a landing pad for it to take hold, some need a little push, and some need a lot of rocket fuel to break the gravitational pull of your old habits. That's OK. Do what you need to do to get that new habit locked and loaded. Ya, it's worth the effort.

Return from Fantasy Island

Part of your aftercare is about believing in yourself, because the light of the next day can make it seem like you just stepped off the plane from Fantasy Island and nothing you experienced was real. C'mon, aliens? Past lives? Angels and goddesses? Hooks and drains from your coworkers? To be honest, the next day it sounds kinda hokey to us healers too, but we know something you don't.

We know that even the hokey, woo woo, crazy-train healings we help facilitate are just the candy coating on the energy you shifted. So many times we don't have words for what we experience in the Akashic realm. There are energies and ideas that defy language, but they need to heal and evolve, too. Even though we don't have the language to express it, we fit it into our realm through stories to help us make sense of it.

Go ahead and relax about the story you got in your healing. You don't have to put on an aluminum foil hat to avoid alien death rays, or sprinkle holy water on your boss who looked like a demon in your healing. You can return from Fantasy Island and understand that it is all a metaphor. Well, most of it. Artists understand this concept; they demonstrate this through their paints, images, and harmonies. They know there are no words for their creation, there is only the creation of the energy they are communicating; the interpretation is up to the observer.

Think about the most beautiful sunset you have ever experienced; the emotion, the colors, the sounds and smells. It would take a novel's worth of writing to fully express that sunset, and still it would not fully translate. It would only feel like you were able to express that moment when you find someone who could relate to that story, who had an experience to match it. That is the story of your Akashic healing—you need a story to match the energy so you can understand the lesson later. So, go ahead and embrace the story and make it home from Fantasy Island.

Getting Everyone on the Same Page

We guarantee the people around you will react in varying degrees to your healing. Even though you have sent out the karmic memo to all the players in your healing, they may not have been able to integrate it yet, so don't be surprised at a little pushback on your newly healed energy. It's OK. Just remember that they have their own journey and their own process, so keep steady with your new energy.

It is true that when you change from within, the world changes around you to make way for your new healing; but you may just have a few stragglers. When you are confronted with a surprising and unexpected negative response from the people in your life, it is best to remember not to take it personally. You just flipped the script on them, and they are still responding to the old you and need time to catch up. In the meantime, there are a few things to ask yourself as you lock your healing in place and avoid regressing to old behaviors:

* Is this just a reaction to my healing?
* Is this reaction about me or them?
* What is the new habit I am engaging in?
* Do I need to respond to this?
* I release this person from my energy, and I release the energy of their reaction back to the earth.

Healings that involve your reactions or relationships to other people can be very freeing for both parties. When you clear the karmic story that you were fulfilling together, you get a chance to see if there is a better relationship under all the garbage. Either way, you are free to upgrade your relationships.

🖋 Akashic Tales from Aunt Jacki

I cleared a big karmic issue where I kept trying to heal my relationship with my mother through my female friendships. I made a lot of mistakes in picking friends and ruined some friendships because I responded to my friend like I would to my mother. After I worked on clearing layers of that one healing session at I time, I had a big argument with a close friend. It was a worthy argument—my feelings were hurt, and I decided to argue it out rather than walk away. At the end of the discussion we both asked each other where we stood, and both of our responses were "I think this friendship is strong enough to handle an argument, don't you?" This was actually a new script for both of us, and we have a deeper friendship now.

Letting Go of the Past

There is a societal belief that the past defines us. We think we are our cultural nationality, our family economic structure, the race of our ancestors, the neighborhood we grew up in, our childhood experiences, and the job we just left. All of these connections and experiences become our history. Whether they are good or bad experiences, they are the story of us. Sometimes the story rings true for us, and sometimes it makes us slide right off our path.

Thankfully, that story is not static, but dynamic. Think about how many times it has changed. For Jacki it's about how many fashion incarnations she has gone through. (She defines periods in her life based on her fashion trend at the time.) Seeing life as fluid is an important part of being able to let go and allow change. Look at your childhood. Were you known as a quiet child, or a mouthy one? Were you the prom queen or the geek? Those labels come out of specific circumstances, and as we grow up, we can drop the labels and forget all about them (until the family or class reunion).

When you decide to let go of the past and actually do it, others will be able to let go, too. So if you are still carrying those labels throughout adulthood, it's time to do some healing and let it go.

No matter what the problem is or where the issue is rooted—in a past life, a family legacy, identity issues, or anger at another—if you decide that it's a valued part of your script, it can be difficult to fully let it go. What we have found is that you have to understand the pain or reward of this part of your issue. We have to tell on your ego again. It's your ego that hangs on to this story, even though it is painful, because there is some reward there. There is a boost to your importance when it knows there is going to be a prize for suffering so, and the ego sees this as good. It really thinks you'll improve your overall chances of being the big kahuna if you work that victim tagline just right. It's a survival mechanism, and you have to find the story and rewrite it. When you do that, the past is so easy to let go of.

✒ Aunt Jacki's Tales of White-Knuckling Her Past

I was married once before. I met him when I was seventeen and he was thirty-seven. I was with him for eight plus years total, and most of it was a nightmare. Today he is in prison—game over.

I used to tell the details of my life with him to every new friend. It wasn't right away, but they would eventually know this about me. I was keeping the past in the present, and it was defining me. It kept leaking through and blocking different issues in my life. Eventually, I realized that this story had become a badge of honor for me. When I told this story, I got sympathy and validation as to how strong I am to have survived that time in my life. My ego loved that, and to have the strokes I was required to keep the pain too. That was my pain or reward. When I let go of that identity need, I was able to let go of the past.

To let go of the past and the pain it brought, you have to let go of the reward your ego is hanging on to. It's OK to not be defined by this anymore, as you have a lot of amazing things coming up in your future that are much more worthy of you. If you find you are having a hard time letting something drop and be done with it, you will probably find you have a soul part invested in this event or circumstance. Please refer to working with healing soul parts in chapter 9.

Blister Pack Exercise

It is fairly common to have a reaction to your own Akashic session the day after or when you get back to the real world. When this starts to happen, you can quickly go back into your records and ask the keeper to blister pack this reaction for you so you can review and heal at a more opportune time (and not when you are trying to talk to your boss).

Excuse yourself from whatever situation you are in and find a private spot (a bathroom trip is a great private place, or in your car). Take three slow, deep breaths, each one slower than the last. Take three more slow, deep breaths until you can count to five on each inhale and exhale.

Let your shoulders drop and relax; wiggle your toes and your eyebrows to release tension at your root and at your crown. Visualize this reaction you are having in your mind's eye. It could look like anything, or feel like anything. If you have to, use your imagination to draw a picture of it. Don't worry about stepping back into your Akashic records, you are already there with the reaction you are having.

Now, start rolling up that image into a tighter and tighter ball. Ask for help from your Akashic record keepers to make that as small as possible. Ask them for any messages to help you let go of this reaction you are having right now. Breathe slowly and just let the answers come without judgment.

Now ask your keepers to seal this issue in a clear, hard blister pack that is difficult to open. Tell them (and yourself) that you will be addressing this issue in the near future and set a date that you will work on this. Visualize the hard blister pack being created around the issue and the pack being stored in your records for the next time you go in.

It is important that you look at it again. If you let it just fester in your records, it may become a bigger issue than it initially was, as it will piggyback on similar events as they come up for you.

Write down your observation on the issue and use those notes the next time you go into the Akasha.

Now gather your energy up; fill yourself and all the empty spots in your energy field that were created by this reaction. Ask your higher self to send in more of your own essence to strengthen yourself.

Give yourself some much-needed appreciation, and visualize yourself settling into your body; your nose in your nose and your toes in your toes.

Use the Processes or Don't—
Your Akashic Records Still Rock!

The sisters of Akashic anarchy can be a bit hypocritical. First we tell you to do as you will in your records; go get them, they are yours. Now we show you a method of how to work with your records full of steps, rules, and regulations. So which is it?

It's both. There will be times when you peek in, kick some Akashic ass, and go on with your day. Then there are times when the big issues come up and feel overwhelming. Some of you want to freestyle your healings in the records, while others need a process. We have experienced all of that and more. We started our Akashic journey freestyling a hit-or-miss jumble of actions, and we have to say that we missed quite a bit when we got in over our heads. The Akashic Wisdom Process was about us putting a rhythm to our healings to make sure they were all wrapped up in a nice neat bow at the end.

Try it both ways, and if you get stuck, get inspired by following the Rhythm Method or the Akashic Wisdom Process. Either way you'll impress yourself and become wiser at the same time.

Go Forth and Heal and Grow!

We've laid out our way of working within the records; now all that is left is to do it. Start your path, make mistakes, and plan on washing, rinsing, and repeating whatever mysteries you are solving. Find courage, dig deep, and believe in yourself. You have permission. To paraphrase Glinda the Good Witch of the North, "You have had the power all along."

Trailblazers of the Akasha Craze

In other Akashic record books you will find a detailed history of the Akashic records studies. Since we didn't go this route for our own exploration of the Akashic records, we can't speak from experience of how all of these mystics contributed to the Akashic record craze, but we can give you a quick rundown if you want to explore them for yourself.

* Alice Bailey (1880–1949) was a member of the Theosophical Society and author of twenty-two books on metaphysics, including yogic practices. Bailey made a connection to the Akashic records in her book *The Light of the Soul,* where she writes: "Knowledge of previous incarnations becomes available when the power to see thought images is acquired." Sounds like the Akashic records to us!

* Helena Petrovna Blavatsky (1831–91), founder of the Theosophical Society, wrote extensively about the Akasha and believed that we should all learn to access the Akashic records.

* Edgar Cayce (1877–1945), known as the sleeping prophet, referenced the Akashic records as the Book of Life and God's Book of Remembrance.

* Levi H. Dowling (1844–1911), author of the Aquarian Gospel, stated that he transcribed it directly from the Book of Remembrance.

* Charles Leadbeater (1854–1934), another member of the Theosophical Society, wrote extensively about the difference between the astral plane and the Akashic records in hopes

that his teachings would help us avoid getting tangled up in the astral plane and assuming that we'd arrived.

* Henry Steele Olcott (1832–1907), military officer, lawyer, and journalist, was the first American Buddhist, and cofounder and first president of the Theosophical Society. Olcott documented many of H. P. Blavatsky's explorations of the Akashic records.

* Rudolf Steiner (1861–1925), was for a time a student of H. P. Blavatsky. His experience with the Akashic records, which he called the Akashic Chronicle, is well-documented.

Glossary

Astral Plane

The astral plane is a dimension that lies just outside our daily reality. It is where we store our emotions, hopes, fears, and intentions that cannot be processed by our conscious mind, similar to the unconscious mind in that it holds the junk that we throw off through negative or overwhelming reactions. The astral plane is not the same as the Akashic records. The only thing you'll find in the astral realm is space junk.

Blister Pack

A blister pack is a creative spiritual tool that contains any issues that cannot be addressed in the current healing session. It will limit or block the issues' potential negative interference with daily life.

Divine Ally

A divine ally is any spiritual helper that is not an ancestor who works with you in a higher spiritual vibration to heal, illuminate, and evolve your spirit.

The Divine

The Divine is an all-encompassing term to describe the chosen higher power of our readers.

Ego

The ego is the self-esteem or self-image of any person, the sense of "I" that allows her to distinguish herself from others in her daily reality or spiritual life. The ego is a Freudian term that regulates the communication between the primal and logical parts of the personality.

Hero

The hero takes on many forms, from a comic book character to someone in your life who has behaved in a heroic way that you admire. The hero represents that energy needed to bring selfless courage to a difficult healing crisis.

Higher Self

Your higher self is the part of you that is in direct connection with the Divine. It interfaces with the Divine to contain and then transmit the perfect amount and kind of light to animate, inspire, and heal your physical body, mind, and soul. This part of you is unchanged by your soul's human or physical experiences; rather, it directs and guides the soul through its experiences. It is the guiding light that never changes and holds your true identity and essence intact while you incarnate and have adventures.

The Light

The Light is the current metaphysical term used when discussing the energy that loves, heals, teaches, and creates. God is light.

Oversoul

Your soul deposits the experiences of its lifetime in a repository called an oversoul. The oversoul will incarnate many projections of itself to collect as many experiences as possible for learning and enlightenment. These projections are called souls, and there is typically one soul per incarnation.

Past Life

Based on the belief of reincarnation, a past life is where a part of your soul existed and experienced a reality in a different time or era than the present.

Past Self

A past self represents an earlier time in your current life when you dealt with things differently than you do now. When you regress to meet a younger you, you are meeting a past self.

Sea of Souls

Based on the West African cosmology that eventually became Santeria, this is a belief that all souls upon death become part of a sea of souls. A new soul is born from the sea as a completely new soul.

Shadow Self

The shadow self is where aspects of our personality we are unconscious of or disapproving of reside. This is considered the dark or primitive aspect of the ego. We are often afraid of our own shadow self.

Spiritual Habits

A spiritual habit is behavior we unconsciously do repeatedly as a response to a spiritual stimulus. This behavior can be creative or destructive.

Transmutational Energy

Known as the violet flame, transmutational energy lifts dense, heavy energy to vibrate faster. This speeding up of energy heals the physical body, balances emotions, and opens the mind to receive spiritual intelligence. We use the violet flame to help clear toxic energy in our lives and in our Akashic records.

About the Authors

Photo by Sherry Kruzman-Martin

Jacki Smith and Patty Shaw have been sisters all of Jacki's life. Patty hung out with their other six siblings before Jacki showed up, and they have been best buds ever since.

Jacki lives in southeast Michigan with her husband and daughter, where she runs three businesses, teaches classes, consults spiritually, hosts "Keep it Magic Radio," and runs amok. Coventry Creations is her life's work, as she has spent twenty-plus years dedicated to making magic happen every day.

Patty lives with her husband and cat in the southeast area of the Michigan mitten. She is the chief candle goddess at Coventry Creations and an author, teacher, Reiki master, healer, and all-around saint (her staff elected her to that office). Patty is also cofounder of the School of Akashic Healing, where she trains others in the Akashic healing methods.

You can contact both Jacki and Patty through *www.coventry creations.com*, where you can book an Akashic record healing session with either sister.

To Our Readers

Weiser Books, an imprint of Red Wheel/Weiser, publishes books across the entire spectrum of occult, esoteric, speculative, and New Age subjects. Our mission is to publish quality books that will make a difference in people's lives without advocating any one particular path or field of study. We value the integrity, originality, and depth of knowledge of our authors.

Our readers are our most important resource, and we appreciate your input, suggestions, and ideas about what you would like to see published.

Visit our website at *www.redwheelweiser.com* to learn about our upcoming books and free downloads, and be sure to go to *www.redwheelweiser.com/newsletter* to sign up for newsletters and exclusive offers.

You can also contact us at *info@rwwbooks.com* or at

Red Wheel/Weiser, LLC
665 Third Street, Suite 400
San Francisco, CA 94107